PSYCHOLOGICAL SERVICES
FOR
SCHOOLS

PSYCHOLOGICAL SERVICES

FOR

SCHOOLS

Edited by

W. D. WALL

WASHINGTON SQUARE · 1956

NEW YORK UNIVERSITY PRESS

FOR UNESCO INSTITUTE FOR EDUCATION

First published 1956
by Unesco Institute for Education
First United States edition 1956

Manufactured by Drukkerij Holland N.V., Amsterdam

FOREWORD

This report on Psychological Services in Schools is the third of a series published by the Unesco Institute for Education.

The Institute was glad to organise this conference of experts in cooperation with Unesco. Dr. W. D. Wall, of Unesco, was the originator of the enterprise. With his help and through his intimate and wide-spread knowledge of the subject, together with his energy, the conference proved to be a success. The Institute further expresses its thanks to Dr. Wall for the untiring way in which he has worked as editor in the compilation of this report.

In some European countries the scope and the aims of educational psychology are still questions under discussion. This report may help to clarify the field, and it is certainly of some value in so far as, from an international aspect, it gives exact information and attempts to systematize the rich material which is available.

WALTHER MERCK

CONTENTS

CONTENTS

PREFATORY NOTE

In November-December 1952, Unesco convened a small expert conference on Education and the Mental Health of Children in Europe. This conference marked the beginning of a considerable series of activities pursued by Unesco itself and by a number of voluntary or official bodies with which Unesco cooperates. Among the many topics raised but not fully dealt with by this conference, was the whole large and important question of how the modern sciences of child study and educational psychology could be brought into more effective relation with the work of European schools; and how, for those countries whose educational systems are rapidly developing, the European experience might be made available as a guide to avoiding some at least of the errors and hesitations which have marked educational development in this matter since the turn of the present century.

The Unesco Institute for Education, Hamburg, agreed that this was a topic which entered into its terms of reference. Accordingly a small preparatory meeting of distinguished German educators, psychologists, psychiatrists, and of members of the Institute staff and of Unesco Secretariat was convened in Hamburg to discuss the best way of treating this matter. It was decided that a small expert study group should be asked to consider in a practical fashion, the principles, objectives, and the basic planning governing the structure of a service of psychology for schools and other educational institutions. Such a study could not enter into details which depend upon the administrative structure of each country nor should it lose itself in the discussion of theoretical problems. It should be based on current practice and suggest ways in which existing services might be made more comprehensive or, where no services exist, the lines on which they might be profitably developed. Other than the enquiry made by the International Bureau of Education in 1948,[1] very little up-to-date information was available. Moreover, since the expert group was to think out

1. *School Psychologists*, Geneva and Paris, IBE-Unesco, No. 105, 1948.

9

afresh the part that applied psychology might play in education, information was necessary concerning methods and organizations not narrowly classifiable as "psychological services" or "child guidance clinics", projets for the future, and an assessment of needs not as yet being met.

Accordingly, the Secretariat of Unesco drew up a detailed study plan which was sent to the National Commissions for Unesco in European countries, to national organizations active in any part of the field and to individual experts. Information was also sought from each country on the nature and extent of the special educational provision made for various groups of exceptional children. Thus the study group, when it met, had a considerable volume of information at its dispoal, much of it hitherto uncoordinated, all of it rich in practical suggestions as to methods of developing services.

The committee which had planned the broad lines of the study represented most of the disciplines concerned with childhood, and in constituting the expert group the same principle was followed. The United Nations Bureau of Social Affairs, the World Health Organization, and Unesco were represented, and the World Federation for Mental Health—an international non-governmental organization—was also invited to contribute. Among the nineteen participants, who came from seven European countries, there were educators, school medical officers, psychologists, psychiatrists, social workers, administrators and a magistrate, all of them in one way or another directly concerned in their daily practice with the work of the schools, most of them engaged in functioning services or in the training of those who would staff them.

For a week, from April 5 to 10, 1954, in the relaxed and genial atmosphere of the Institute, the group discussed a very broad agenda under the able direction of its Chairman, the Lady Norman. No lectures were given nor papers read; the whole meeting proceeded by the quick give-and-take of discussion without sidestepping the many difficult interprofessional issues which such a subject presents and without resting until a reasonable and workable agreement was reached. In the evenings and at other times individuals or small subcommissions wrote the first rough drafts for the report.

It is on the basis of these drafts that Part III of this book was written. A connected manuscript was prepared and certain gaps were made good. This was then circulated to each participant, who was invited to comment upon it, to suggest new formulations, deletions or additions. All the comments were incorporated in the final version which, in spite perhaps of some repetitions, some inevitable generalities and a good many compromises, now represents a brief statement of the collective thinking of the study group, rather than what any one member of it might have written if left to himself.

The original intention had been to publish nothing more than the report with a selected bibliography. However it was felt that the information received from representative European countries giving a picture of different conceptions in the development of psychological services would round out and complete the report and give practical illustration to some of its principles. Similarly the historical development in Europe of various forms of educational and child guidance sheds some light upon current practices as well as indicating how clearly pioneers foresaw the needs which today we are only just beginning to meet.

The task of writing these two parts was delicate. The studies of the ten countries which form Part II of this book were based upon the documents and other material acknowledged in the text. Selection, rearrangement and condensation were however inevitable, with the danger of giving a falsified picture. Each section therefore was resubmitted for comments to those who had supplied the original material. While none is complete in every detail and all, to those who are intimately acquainted with the country, must seem impressionistic, they give between them an overview of the situation as it is now in 1955.

The historical introduction which forms Part I has the purpose of putting into perspective the main ideas which have prepared the way for what we have today. Though the account has drawn heavily on already published sources, it is not to be expected that all will agree with the interpretation of the facts as they are given; but, again, in spite of an element of condensation inevitable in so short a work, the attempt has been made to select the significant facts and to stress particularly those elements of thinking and development which seem most likely to be fruitful for current and future advances in the use of psychology as one of the basic sciences of education.

In the summer of 1954, as a direct outcome of the work of the expert group, the American Psychological Association invited Dr. W. D. Wall to take part in its "Work Conference on the Selection and Training of School Psychologists". It was thus possible to put at the disposal of our American colleagues the thinking and experience of European educators and psychologists, and in some small way repay the debt which Europe owes to American educational psychology.

This introductory note should end with a word of thanks to the Institute and to its staff. Their aid during the meeting itself, in the preliminary planning and right to the day when this book is published has been unobtrusive but invaluable. The house in Feldbrunnenstrasse, Hamburg, is something more than a neutral meeting place; it exerts a catalytic influence on those who meet there and ensures that the cooperation engendered by working together round a table shall continue when each participant has returned to his country. It is from this continued participation that anything of value which appears in the following pages has been drawn.

PART I

EXISTING CONCEPTIONS AND SERVICES IN EUROPE[1]

HISTORICAL INTRODUCTION[2]

The practical application of psychology to the problems of the schools is relatively recent. It is only within the last threequarters of a century that anything approaching a coherent science of Child Study has begun to develop, and the foundations of a scientific psychology of education are more recent still. Nevertheless, the conception of Child Guidance as a service of expert advice to parents, teachers and children themselves in the best ways of directing or re-directing the child's mental development has been a feature of educational writing for many centuries. In the works of Plato, Castiglione, Ascham, Comenius, Rousseau, Pestalozzi and Froebel, to name but a few, will be found explicitly stated the notions of education and educational method as constructive processes of guidance aimed to help each child achieve the fullest possible expansion of his personality and the fullest realization of his potentialities. Though the current jargon is not used, "Child Guidance", "Preventive Mental Hygiene" and a great many other ideas which underlie our modern attempts to apply educational psychology to the improvement of the education of the individual child, preceded, sometimes by centuries, the development of the scientific knowledge necessary to implement them.

Scientific child study, the parent of educational psychology, is a science which owes little to that "general psychology"

1. Certain sections of this paper, in a somewhat different and more condensed form have already appeared as a contribution to the *Year Book of Education 1955*, London. Evans Bros, 1955 (see Wall, W. D. "Guidance Services in Europe" pp. 578–602).

2. For much of the material on which this section is based, I am indebted to Keir, G. "The History of Ghild Cuidance". *Brit. Journ. Ed. Psych. Vol. XXII, Pt.* 1. Feb. 1952, and Flügel, J. C., *A Hundred Years of Psychology*, 1833–1933, 2nd edition, London, Duckworth, 1951, 424 pp., and to the helpful comments of Sir Cyril Burt, who read the manuscript.

which was the offspring of philosophy or to the physiological psychologists led by Wundt who concentrated upon a man as a neurological mechanism. Its origins are to be found in the work of the evolutionary biologists of the latter half of the nineteenth century. In 1877, Darwin published in *Mind* his "Biographical Sketch of an Infant", a work based upon careful and objective observation, which was hailed by Taine as "pointing the way to a new field of science". Similar studies followed: by Perez (1878, 1886), Compayre (1893) and Queval (1893) in France, and by Preyer (1882) in Germany. On the continent, the work of Herbert Spencer had an even greater influence than in Britain. Taine's book on *Intelligence*, avowedly an attempt to state the Spencerian point of view, was the starting point for the later work of Binet. These studies emphasing as they did the biological nature of man gave the beginnings of an empirical foundation to the view points expressed both by Bain and by Spencer twenty years earlier.[1]

In 1884, Francis Galton opened his anthropometric laboratory and laid the foundations of the mental testing movement and of much else beside. Galton advocated the study of the individual child with a view to practical recommendations about his treatment at home, at school, and as an aid to subsequent vocational guidance. He stressed and began to investigate the differences, genetic and environmental, between individuals; and his laboratory, finally established at University College, London, may be regarded as the earliest psychological service or Child Guidance Centre, antedating by ten years the first similar organization (that of Witmer) across the Atlantic and by more than thirty years the first so-called Child Guidance Clinics.

The notion that psychological differences between children could be scientifically measured and made the basis of practical predictions and recommendations, was enthusiastically taken up by teachers themselves, notably by Dr. Sophie Bryant,[2] a biol-

---

1. Bain, T., *The Senses and the Intellect*, 1855 — *Emotions and the Will*, 1859. Spencer, H., *Principles of Psychology*, 1855.

2. Anthrop, J., *Experiments in testing the Character of School Children*, 1886, Inst. XV.

ogist and headmistress of the Camden High School for Girls, London. Towards the end of the century, Sully, Professor of Mind and Logic at University College, London, opened the first psychological laboratory in Great Britain. It was there that William McDougall, his Assistant and Director of the Laboratory, began systematic observation and experiments with individual children. Courses were conducted that were attended by school inspectors like Winch, Kimmins and Ballard, the pioneers of those steady attempts at the reform of English education to make it more child-centred, which took place in the first decades of the twentieth century.

As a result of this and much other activity led principally by Galton and Sully, the *British Child Study Association* was founded in 1893 with the support of London teachers, inspectors and education officials. One of its primary objects was "to study the normal as well as the abnormal, paying special attention to the investigation of the commoner cases of minor deviations among normal children, as well as to the diagnosis of the rarer abnormal or pathological types". Sully contended that "medical science is more familiar with the rare but striking cases of mental disease and defect; mental science, on the other hand, though it has learned much from the suggestive analogies that may be drawn, has already shown that during childhood at least, the vast majority of cases consist of deviations *within* the normal range rather than aberrations *from* the normal.[1] "Hence", he added "we need a new kind of specialist—a psychological specialist in fact" who should have a gift of sympathetic insight and a specific psychological training based upon a knowledge of general psychology and methodical practice in the application of the scientific methods of psychology to the study of individual children.[2]

The foundation of the Child Study Association in London was followed by the establishment of branches elsewhere and by the

1. *The Teacher's Handbook of Psychology*, 1886 — *The Human Mind*, 1892.
2. Sully, J. "The Service of Psychology to Education" *Am. Ed. Review IV*, 1892.

inclusion of courses in "Child Psychology", "Individual Psychology" and the like in the syllabuses of University departments of Education and Philosophy. A centre like that of Galton was begun under McDougall's influence at Oxford and later (1907) Burt, a pupil of McDougall, started similar work in Liverpool with the co-operation and support of the education authority and the courts. Six years later (1913) on the initiative of school inspectors and of the Child Study Association, the London County Council set up within its Education Department the first official psychologists' office, and Cyril Burt was appointed as psychologist to the Education Authority.

From the commencement of his work in Liverpool, Burt devoted his attention to research into all the practical problems of the schools and especially to an exploration of the psychology of individual differences so important for the adaptation of education to the rhythms of child growth. As early as 1903, he was devising measures of higher cognitive processes through tests of Opposites, Analogies, Syllogistic reasoning and the like —types of test which still hold the field as the best measures of verbal intelligence. In 1911[1] he advocated the combination of such tests into a group test of general intelligence. He thus carried Galton's work further and laid the foundation of the mental measurement movement as applied to education. From the date of his appointment to the London County Council, his "Reports of the Psychologist to the London Council" begin to cover all the practical aspects of a functioning service as we now come to know them.[2] He devised individual and group tests of educational attainment, and investigated the distribution and relations of educational abilities among school children, concerning himself with educational and vocational guidance;

1.   Burt, C., "Experimental Tests of Higher Mental Processes and their Relation to General Intelligence". *J. Exp. Ped.* Vol. 1., 1911. See also Yerkes, R. M., (ed.) "Psychological Examining in the US Army" — *Memoirs of the Academy of Science*, Vol. 15, Government Printing Office, 1921.

2.   *Reports of the Psychologist to the London County Council*, P. S. King & Son, London, 1913-30. A complete bibliography of Burt's work will be found in Hannah Steinberg "List of Publications by Sir Cyril Burt" *Brit. Journ. Ed. Psych., Vol. XXI. Pt. 1.*, Feb. 1951.

and began his classical studies of backward children and of young delinquents. From the early twenties, the influence of his empirical studies and still more of his capacity at once to develop a theoretical basis for child study and to express this in practical educational terms, began to influence the official publications of the Board of Education.[1]

Burt's various contributions to the development of psychological services in England are difficult to overestimate. Perhaps in the long run his broad methodological contribution will prove to be the most valuable. From the outset he combined the observational case study method with group studies firmly based in an experimental and statistical framework. He set the abnormal individual against a background of normal growth and development; and his two great works on the *Backward Child* and the *Young Delinquent* are a masterly demonstration of the value of control groups in any investigation of human psychological characteristics. The service which he created set a pattern of close co-operation with the schools, of investigation by rigorous scientific methods of the practical problems of education, of the treatment of individual cases and of the integration under the guidance and inspiration of the Psychologist's office of the many special educational facilities of a large authority—a pattern which still dominates the best services in England.

Burt's work, first in Liverpool and then in London, was so successful that similar methods were adopted in many other areas both in England (Leicester and Stafford) and in Scotland (Edinburgh, Glasgow and Aberdeen). It was not until after the first world war, seven years after Burt's appointment to the L.C.C. and thirteen years after he had begun his work in Liverpool, that Crichton Miller established the Institute of Medical Psychology, subsequently renamed the Tavistock Clinic. Later

1. Board of Education (U.K.) Report on *Psychological Tests of Educable Capacity* HMSO 1924. *Report of Joint Committee of Board of Education and Board of Control on Mental Deficiency*. HMSO 1929 (chapters on "The Nature of Mental Defect", "The Classification of Mental Defectives" and an Appendix on "Mental and Educational Tests"), Board of Education *Report on Infant and Nursery Schools*. HMSO 1934 (Appendix, with Susan Isaacs, on "Emotional Development up to the age of Seven").

still, the Jewish Health Organization started the East London Clinic under Dr. Emmanuel Miller. Both of these, lacking the close integration with the schools and their problems and the research orientation, at once practical and yet rigorously experimental, which Burt had given to the L.C.C. service, remained essentially psychiatric and preoccupied with the abnormal.

Very similar developments had been taking place in Europe, and especially in France. In 1894, the "*Société libre pour l'Etude de l'Enfant*" was formed in Paris; and shortly afterwards, impressed by the ideas of Galton, Binet published his series of papers on *La Psychologie individuelle*.[1] In 1905, in conjunction with Vaney, he established a "*Pedagogical Laboratory*", and proposed to the Minister of Public Instruction a comprehensive scheme for the examination of subnormal children which included physical, medical, educational and psychological examinations with a report on social conditions. In 1904, he established the first version of his famous intelligence scale. In Germany, Meumann, Stern and Bobertag were also doing much to provide the theoretical background of child psychology and guild guidance. The three volumes of Meumann's lectures on experimental pedagogy (published in 1904) had a profound influence on English work,[2] as well as on work elsewhere.[3] Later Stern's Institute of Applied Psychology and his journal attracted great interest. But practical applications remained at first sporadic and tentative and were in many European countries almost entirely neglected.

In Italy, however, as early as 1899, Sante de Sanctis, recognizing that psychiatry was not the only, or even the most important, discipline involved in the guidance of abnormal children, initiated a cross disciplinary approach. In his *Asili*

1. *Année Psychologique III.* 1896.
2. *Experimental Education* by R. R. Rusk was almost a condensed translation of Meumann.
3. Particularly in Belgium where the Laboratory of Professor Buyse was inspired by Meumann's work. See Wolter, E. *Analyse experimentale du Travail des Ecoliers. La Psychopédagogie d'Ernst Meumann.* Louvain, Nauwelaerts, 1955.

Scuola per Anormali Psichici he instituted a consultation based upon a team which included, as well as the psychiatrist, a specialised teacher, a psychologist and a social worker. Thus by nearly a quarter of a century de Sanctis anticipated the concept of teamwork in the diagnosis and treatment of severely abnormal cases put forward by the proponents of Child Guidance Clinics in the United States. His initiative, however, remained, in spite of the efforts of Montesano, Vidoni, Montessori, Banissoni and Cacchione, without sequel in Italy.

In Switzerland,[1] a more propitious start was made. In 1900, Claparède interested himself, at the demand of a young teacher, in the educational problems of a class of subnormal children. In 1904, in the *Signal de Genève* he published a series of articles on "La Psychologie de l'enfant et la Pédagogie expérimentale" —the first sketch of his book of the same title which appeared in 1916. In 1906, he began his *"Séminaire de Psychologie pédagogique"* which was ambitiously planned to cover practical educational psychology, physiology, the health of the school child, and the pathology of childhood. At first it was accepted as part of the course of teacher training but after a year had to be abandoned, to the great regret of the practising teachers of Geneva, because of opposition from the Faculties of Arts, Science and Medicine.

However, undaunted, Claparède in conjunction with Bouvier, Milliourd and Pierre Bovet opened in 1912 the "Ecole des Sciences de l'Education", later the "Institut des Sciences de l'Education" at Geneva. Space does not permit full justice being done to the immense contribution of the Institut to the development of experimental education and child study. To it however we owe much of the dynamic of educational reform in the first decades of the century and, through the International Bureau of Education its later offshoot, many contemporary concepts of international technical co-operation in the field of education. From the outset, Claparède and his remarkable collaborators foresaw that the basis of the sciences of education

1.   See Bovet, P., *Cinquante ans de l'Institut Jean-Jacques Rousseau*

was child study in all its aspects, and that training must go hand in hand with functioning services and continuing research. Consequently the years from 1912 onwards saw the training of teachers, psychologists, social workers and specialised educators of many kinds grow alongside a programme of basic research in most of the aspects of child psychology, educational psychology and scientific pedagogy. Particularly of interest in the present context were the *consultation médico-pédagogique* and the *Cabinet d'orientation professionnelle*. The latter, inspired by developments in Belgium, concentrated upon the twin aspects— that of a psycho-social case study of the individual child and that of the detailed psychological study of each vocation. The former, established in 1913, was preoccupied from the outset with all those problems of a child's growth which might interfere with his educational progress. Quite early in its existence, it experimented with parent education, an initiative subsequently developed by the Ecole du Mail, and, from 1916 onwards, had associated with it, special remedial classes for retarded children.

Claparède's initiatives were not without official sequels. In 1920, Hegg established in Berne under the Department of Education of the city, *La consultation pédagogique de la ville de Berne*. Eight years later, a school psychological service which included in its functions problems of delinquency and of vocational guidance, as well as a considerable task of public education, was begun in Basle—roughly contemporary with the *Laboratoire de pédagogie et de psychologie de l'enfant* at Angleur in Belgium.[1]

In America, Stanley Hall, recently returned from Wundt's laboratory at Leipzig, founded in 1891 the *Pedagogical Seminary*, the first journal devoted to educational psychology and child study. In 1904, he published his great work on *Adolescence* which is remarkable for the number of empirical studies on which it is based and for its insistence on the genetic, biological approach. J. M. Cattell, who had studied in England under

1. For a description of these services see pp. 45–46 (Angleur) p. 77 (Berne).

Galton, encouraged his pupil Witmer in 1896 to open a "Psychological clinic"[1] at Pennsylvania University. Meanwhile another of Cattell's pupils, E. L. Thorndike, published his *Educational Psychology* for long a standard text book. Baldwin in 1921 published the first of the University of Iowa studies in Child Welfare on "The Physical Growth of Children from Birth to Maturity".[2] In the main, however, the American psychologists, under the influence of Titchener and Watson, remained strongly attached to the intellectualistic and associationist standpoint, ignoring or explicitly rejecting the emphasis on the child's emotional life, upon education, and upon the influence of unconscious motives. It is not surprising therefore that in the earlier American clinics, the function of the pychologist came to be identified almost entirely with the application of intellectual and educational tests. It was the leading psychiatrist of his day, Adolf Meyer, who, incorporating much of the thinking of the British biological school, and of the views of Janet and Freud, termed his field of work "psychobiology". In 1909, a year after Burt had begun his studies of adolescent delinquents in Liverpool, Healy, a pupil of J. M. Cattell and William James, and a follower of Meyer, began his study of delinquents in Illinois. In the same year, Beers founded the *National Committee for Mental Hygiene*. This latter in the early nineteen-twenties turned its attention from conditions in mental hospitals to the psychiatric study of delinquent and difficult children and with financial support from the Commonwealth Fund set up a number of "Child Guidance Clinics" to combat delinquency.

It was not until 1928 that, financed by the Commonwealth Fund, the first so-called "Child Guidance Clinic" was set up outside the United States—in England. Originally, at the suggestion of Burt and Nunn, this was intended to provide the widest form of psychological service to schools, parents, teachers and children and not merely to concentrate upon the treatment

1. This clinic directed its efforts to the "whole child" but concentrated largely upon educational problems and Witmer developed his concept of diagnostic teaching there.
2. University of Iowa, *Studies in Child Welfare, Vol. I.*, Nov. 1921.

and prevention of delinquency or upon "problem children". It thus represented a step forward on the original American conception; it bore an interesting resemblance to Claparède's consultation in Geneva, and embodied the fruits of the experience already gained by Burt under the L.C.C. Early in 1932 however this demonstration clinic became a separate entity from the Child Guidance Council and developed a narrower pattern in which a sharp distinction was made between the functions of psychiatrist and psychologist, a movement away from the European conception towards the then current American one. As the Director, Dr. W. Moodie,[1] stated it, psychology was considered to consist of knowledge of the "structure and operation of intelligence" and psychiatry claimed to consist of "knowledge of the essential mechanisms involved in all forms of behaviour, normal as well as abnormal". This led to an attempt to limit the psychologist's functions to the application of intelligence and educational tests together with the coaching of children experiencing difficulty in any school subject. The study of the affective and conational aspects—that is of the emotional life, the evaluation of behaviour and the study of personality as a whole—was held by Dr. Moodie to be the province of the psychiatrist.

It need perhaps hardly be said that no leading psychologist in England ever accepted this view. But the fact that it could be and still is put forward in Europe and elsewhere, illustrates one of the major points of disagreement within the guidance movement itself in most countries, a difference of view which has given rise to different conceptions of work, to differently stated objectives, to differences of structure and staffing as well as to certain interprofessional tensions. The more moderate views put forward by most of the writers taking part in the recent symposium in the British Journal of Educational Psychology,[2]

1. *Child Guidance by Team Work*, Child Guidance Council, London, 1931.
2. "Symposium on Psychologists and Psychiatrists in the Child Guidance Service", *Brit. Journ. Ed. Psych. Vols. XXI-XXIII*, 1951-53 and especially

by the Committee on Clinical Psychology of the Group for the Advancement of Psychiatry of the American Psychiatric Association,[1] and by the Conference on Graduate Education in Clinical Psychology held at Boulder, Colorado, 1949,[2] have done much to smooth the passage towards effective collaboration. Moreover, as the various professions concerned, become themselves better trained, gain greater insight into the complexity of the problems involved and into the nature of each others' competencies, and learn by experience of working together, relationships at the personal and local levels have improved markedly.

THE MAIN TRENDS OF DEVELOPMENT

There still remain however fundamental differences of emphasis, on both the practical and theoretical levels, and it is probable that the future lies with a combination of types of service or with a service which is genuinely polyvalent. After somewhat more than a half century of research, we still lack adequate surveys of the needs of communities, of schools, of children and of their parents; our knowledge of child development, of the psychology of the educational process, and of the nature and causes of maladjustment is incomplete and for a large part unsystematised. This accounts both for some of the heat which is generated in discussions as to the functions of various services, and for the variety of types of guidance service and their experimental nature.

Most services have grown up in response to a felt need; and the demands have arisen independently in a variety of circum-

the paper by Moody, R. L., "A conflict of disciplines and personalities" and the summing up by Burt.

1. *The Relation of Clinical Psychology to Psychiatry*, G.A.P. Report No. 10, Topeka Kansas, July, 1942.

2. *Training in Clinical Psychology*, Edited by Rannig, Victor, C., New-York, Prentice Hall, 1950. p. 100 and Chapter 13. See also the articles by Akakow, D. "Psychology and Psychiatry". *Am. Journ. Orthopsychiatry*, April and July, 1949. See also Cutts N. E. (ed.) *School Psychologists at Mid-Century*, Washington D. C., American Psychological Association, 1955.

stances. Historically the first and in many ways the most extensive needs are those experienced by the schools. The teacher confronts, daily, problems of intellectual and other differences among his pupils, the difficulties of the dull or abnormal child, the failure of a child who is backward in one subject or technique, aberrations of behaviour towards the too aggressive or the too submissive extremes. As educational systems provide more opportunities of choice, the guidance of pupils becomes more and more necessary; and at the end of full time schooling, there are the problems of vocational guidance and integration into working life. In daily and prolonged contact with a considerable sample of children, the teacher is well placed to carry out guidance, and to detect what is "abnormal" in the sense of unusual. His preoccupation is at once with the development of the individual and with the growth of the whole group emotionally and socially, as well as educationally.

It is not surprising therefore that the educator insists primarily upon the guidance of the normal child, upon the psychology of the educative process and upon the positive use of the school, its methods and its atmosphere to maximize the potentialities of each pupil.[1] The teacher too, by the very nature of his experience, tends to recognize how wide are the confines of the "normal". It will be remembered that the pioneers of child study, in England, France and Switzerland, and elsewhere, early insisted that aberrations within the normal range are more important numerically and practically than aberrations from the normal. Without unduly minimizing the contribution of psychopathology, it can with some reason be contended that the principal contributions both to the fundamental concepts of guidance, conceived of as implicit in a sound education and in the practice of aiding children to adjust and adapt to their environment, have come from the educators themselves. Most of the basic research and many of the experimental services, have come from professors of education who were psychologists like Nunn and Valentine, from practising teachers and school

1.   See for example, Gal, R. 'L'orientation scolaire,' Presses Universitaires de France, Paris, 1946.

inspectors like Ballard, Sophie Bryant, Cousinet, Ferrière and Freinet, and from the pioneers of scientific child study and the techniques of psychological case work, measurement and research like Binet, Burt, Claparède, Susan Isaacs, Meumann, Piaget, Stern and Wallon.

A second line of approach is more specific and starts from the education of the mentally subnormal. Claparède recalls that it was a demand for help from a teacher of very dull children which set him off on the line of thought which culminated in his courses in educational psychology for teachers. Binet in France, Decroly in Belgium and Montessori in Italy began in much the same way. Medical men had long been interested in children whose intelligence was either so impaired by physical or physiological defect or injury or for some genetic reason so markedly below normal that they could not develop like others. Fairly early the severe cases (idiots and imbeciles) and some of the less severe were segregated in institutions for physical treatment and care; and in many countries this tradition of segregation and of exclusively physical treatment persists. It is only comparatively recently that research with mental tests and the results of specialised education have drawn increasing attention to the fact that *pathologically defective* children are relatively rare and that the vast majority of children who experience severe difficulty in ordinary schools are subnormal in their intellectual functioning rather than defective.[1] They represent deviations within a range of continuously varying differences in intellectual ability which includes the highly intelligent at the other extreme. They are not a group apart. Moreover careful investigation has revealed the existence of a relatively larger group—about 10 per cent of children of school age—whose ability demands a modified curriculum and whose greatest need is for careful educational guidance, without which many develop into emotionally and socially maladjusted individuals or even into delinquents.

From the preoccupation with mental subnormality has arisen

1. Attention should be drawn here to the report on *The Mentally Subnormal Child* (WHO, Geneva, Tech. Rep. Series No. 75) prepared by a joint WHO, Unesco, ILO and UN expert group.

in most European countries a service of special institutions for markedly subnormal, often outside the educational system; and in some—as in France, Holland, the United Kingdom and Switzerland—a system of special schools and classes for the educable subnormal. The practical educational work of Decroly in Belgium, of Descoedres in Switzerland, of Seguin and Itard in France, and the more recent activity of Heilpädagogik, a form of remedial education, under Professor Moor of Zürich, have all contributed to give a considerable impetus to this work and to wider problems of educational method and educational guidance. This, in its most advanced form, is seen in the differentiation of provision which is a growing feature of many educational systems which now tend to include special classes for the dull, for those with educational difficulties of a kind which respond to a brief period of special teaching (classes de rattrapage, opportunity groups, remedial education, and the special classes for those with reading difficulties in the United Kingdom, in Denmark and in Sweden). It should not be forgotten either, that general educational method has gained as much from practices developed first in schools and classes for the subnormal as it has from pioneer work in the nursery, kindergarten and infant schools.

Thus the guidance of the mentally subnormal child, beginning mainly as a means of excluding the "ineducable" from school, on the basis of a medical examination only, based often on so called "stigmata"[1] is becoming less an affair of exclusion, and more a process of global assessment—physical, social, psychological and educational—and of the selection of the appropriate form of educational treatment. Further, though in most countries, practice and administrative provision lag well behind actual knowledge, there is an increasing tendency to see that a

1. "Even as late as 1920 the psychiatric examinations carried out by the school medical officer were generally limited to measuring the size of the skull and inspecting the child for "stigmata of degeneracy", "cranial abnormalities", "nerve signs", "symptoms of malnutrition or other chronic deficiencies"!! Mental symptoms, mental causes, and psychological or social methods of treatment were discussed as the speculative fancies of the layman." Keir, G. Loc. cit. supr. p. 14.

complexity of causes underlies the whole problem of educational maladjustment, and that a great flexibility both in guidance concepts and in provision is necessary.

A similar trend is to be observed in relation to delinquency. More and more in most European countries the courts have tended in the last few decades to seek information on the intellectual, emotional and social circumstances of children and adolescents brought before them and to develop, either under the Home Office (Ministry of the Interior) or under the Ministry of Justice a system of social and remedial services, centres of observation and the like. Earlier conceptions of "moral deficiency" of the "born criminal" marked out like the defective by stigmata[1] have ceded to a less over-simplified theory of multiple causation, of prevention by social, educational and psychological means. The work of Burt in Liverpool and London, begun in 1907, of Healy at the Juvenile Court of Cook County, Illinois, begun in 1909, began to draw attention to the existence not only of psychiatric causes—psychosis, severe neurosis, psychopathic temperament and the like—but to causes related to environment, parental discipline, minor emotional disturbance, educational and vocational failure; and to point out that delinquency was a legal conception which did not correspond to a distinguishable psychological entity. The fact that an adolescent or a child committed what the law regarded as a crime has come slowly to be regarded as an indication that something is wrong with the individual's adjustment. American Child Guidance as embodied in the demonstration clinics, opened in St. Louis and Norfolk in 1923 by the National Committee on Mental Hygiene, and supported by the Commonwealth Fund, was originally essentially aimed at "the psychiatric study of difficult, pre-delinquent and delinquent children in schools and juvenile courts; to develop sound methods of treatment based on such study; and to provide courses of training along sound lines for those qualified and desiring to work in this field".[2] This original idea of a "delinquency clinic" with

1. Lombroso, C., *L'Uomo delinquente*, 4th edition, 1889.
2. *Commonwealth Fund Programme for the Prevention of Delinquency.*

psychotherapy as its only or main method of cure rapidly enlarged in America but was in fact never fully accepted in England or indeed in Europe generally where from the outset stress was laid upon environmental, developmental, educational and social factors in causation and consequently in remedy.

We may just briefly indicate another trend of development, which is the outgrowth from adult psychiatric practice and particularly from the out-patient departments of psychiatric hospitals. Here the influence of the psychobiologic and dynamic schools of psychology and psychiatry has had the effect of turning attention to the importance of experiences in childhood and adolescence in the causation of mental disease, adult psychosis and psychoneurosis. Consequently many such departments began to interest themselves in childhood problems and in not a few cases, in the late twenties and early thirties, established rudimentary services of "child guidance" as a part of their function.

TYPES OF SERVICE

These trends which have not fully converged in Europe, the impulse given to the more psychiatric type of service by the Commonwealth Fund and by the American training received by a number of European psychiatrists, accounts for the variety of concepts, organization, administration and finance that one finds in the whole field of guidance. Fundamental differences of view and preoccupation between the medical and educational professions, problems of jurisdiction between ministries of education, health and social welfare, and the like tend to perpetuate separate and sometimes partial services. In the different European countries some one or two of the kinds of service described below and, in some few, all kinds, exist; and in general where there are adjacent services, functional co-operation is good. Not infrequently however, while in practice differently conceived and staffed services work together, behind

Progress Report. New York. Joint Committee on Methods of Preventing Delinquency, 1926, cited in Witmer, H. op. cit. p. 31.

the scenes administrative and interprofessional struggles hinder the fullest development of genuinely comprehensive guidance for all children.

That which comes nearest to serving the needs of all children at least during school age is the system of the *school psychologist* which is found in some European countries. Under this method of organization, the psychologist, usually an experienced teacher with a considerable further training in educational psychology, has his office in one large school or group of schools (1,000 — 1,500 pupils) to which his attention is exclusively devoted. He acts as adviser to his colleagues and to the Head or Director of the school on all matters which affect the development and progress of the pupils, individually or collectively. Frequently he works alone; in certain countries or circumstances he may have, in addition to his psychological duties, responsibility for a class. Sometimes he has a trained assistant as a secretary-tester. Where there are also school social workers, attendance officers, or welfare officers, they may be integrated into or closely associated with his services. In some cases, the psychologist can count on the services of a school medical officer as well as those of a social worker in his team.

As might be expected from his close association with the schools, and from the relatively small population with which he has to do, the school psychologist has as a primary aim the improvement of the atmosphere of the school, the improvement of methods of teaching, and the guidance and adjustment of the ordinary child. Thus school record cards where they exist are either established and maintained by him or completed under his supervision. Not infrequently educational guidance fades imperceptibly into vocational guidance under this system and the school psychologist conducts the group tests and where necessary the individual tests, on the basis of which he acts as the psychological member of the vocational guidance team. He is also concerned with subnormal, failing, maladjusted, or delinquent children and may undertake individual or group remedial work of various kinds, though usually, at any rate for serious cases, he would call upon outside help. It is he also generally who maintains contacts with the outside agencies who become involved with individual children—with the juvenile courts, the social welfare agencies, psychiatric units and the like—and with the parents. In many ways, notably in the numbers of staff involved if the service is extended on the basis of one psychologist even to 1,000 — 1,500 pupils, this is a solution de luxe.

A second type of solution rather similar to this but more thinly spread is the psychologist's office or Child Guidance *Centre*. The psychologist is not attached to any school or group of schools under this system but provides a service for the educational system of a district. His responsibility administratively is to the Director of Education or other principal local administrator. In its most developed form, this type of service operating from a centre where examination of individual children and remedial work of various kinds can be undertaken, has access to all the educational services of the community. Within its orbit therefore fall not only the work of ameliorating the methods and atmosphere of the ordinary schools, the general guidance both educational and vocational of children of school age, and the examination and treatment of various types of problem children, but also a task of advice and psychological supervision undertaken in all types of special school and class.

It will be noted that the emphasis in this solution, as in that of the school psychologist, is placed upon *constructive* mental health through research into education at home and at school, through the dissemination of information and through preventive and remedial work with individual children undertaken at the earliest possible moment. The "therapy" employed is in general educational and environmental; much of it is undramatic work undertaken slowly to assist the teachers or parents to carry out their task in a more effective fashion, and based upon a relationship of confidence between teachers, parents and psychologist in which the latter is regarded as a friendly consultant rather than an authority from outside taking over a "case".

These solutions are essentially urban and depend for their effectiveness either upon the large school unit or upon a central laboratory or office readily accessible to schools, pupils and parents. In rural districts, in parts of Europe where populations are scattered and the schools small, travelling psychological services have been tried with success. These are based either directly and ad hoc on the school needing help, or operate from a number of part-time centres in different areas. Inevitably such services tend less to stress the needs and guidance of the ordinary child and to undertake more action of a diagnostic, advisory or remedial kind with individual problem children. Because of the large population served, such services can only indirectly undertake such activities as systematic school surveys, experiments with improved educational methods, and general teacher or parent counselling. Nevertheless because they work in the schools themselves, they bring skilled aid to places which would otherwise be inaccessible. Coupled with adequate provision for special boarding schools and hostels, they provide the most effective solutions for areas of scattered population.

In completing this sketch of types of organization and orientation which spring principally from an educational and psychological view-point, we should perhaps mention services with more restricted objectives which in fact undertake guidance in various countries. Many schools and school systems have begun to develop systems of school record cards intended as the basis for the educational guidance of school children. Such cards or cumulative records are not in universal use but will be found in schools in Austria,[1] in parts of France,[2] the United Kingdom,[3] and elsewhere. Frequently they originate from a psychological service or are built on the basis of research in educational psychology, and are intended as an instrument by which the teacher himself may fulfil the many of the tasks of the guidance of his own pupils. A necessary complement is of

1. See for example Lang, L. *Neue Wege*, Österreichischer Bundesverlag für Unterricht, Wissenschaft und Kunst. Vienna. 1952 esp. Ch. I.

2. Circulaire du 25 octobre 1952. "Dossier scolaire" in *l'Enseignement du Second Degré*. Mémoires et Documents scolaires. New Series No. 4, Paris, 1954.

3. See for example the card prepared for the National Foundation for Educational Research (U.K.).

course a serious effort to train teachers in the use of these and other methods of objective child study and observation.

In some countries, specific problems of school adaptation have been made the starting point either for a direct ad hoc action or as an essential part of existing psychological services. Special attention has for example been devoted to certain phases of school life where children, teachers and parents have most need of guidance. Thus in Austria, in Norway and in Sweden, great attention is devoted to determining by tests, observation and other means, each child's readiness to begin formal schooling. In the United Kingdom, particularly since the 1944 Education Act, there has been the tendency to attempt to make of the examination at eleven which comes at the end of the primary period, a means of guidance among alternative types of secondary education rather than an instrument of selection for a particular type. So, too, countries like Belgium, Holland, France, and Yugoslavia, which have highly developed systems of vocational guidance, have tended to push the guidance process further and further back into the child's school life and to recognize effectively that vocational guidance is a continuous process and stems from educational guidance.[1] One of the more interesting examples of this type of thinking is *"Le service d'orientation scolaire et universitaire"* of the French University Statistical Bureau described on pages 58-59. In a somewhat similar way, in Belgium for example, comprehensive types of school psychological service have developed from services of vocational guidance which have come to realise that guidance of a child at one point of his career is dependent for its success on what has happened before and that those cases which give the most difficulty in adolescence are just those which might have been discovered (and remedied) earlier.

The types of organization so far described are mainly educa-

1. This position is very fully put in the Belgian official regulations on Vocational Guidance and Psycho-Medico-Social Centres. It is summarized in *"Note sur l'organisation et le planning du travail"*, Centre Psycho-medico-social d'Etterbeek (mimeographed).

tional in their inspiration and directed more or less broadly to the problems of the schools. Though the distinction is not a sharp one—and as time goes on and experience accumulates the view-points tend to meet and exert a mutual influence—there are also types of organization which are mainly psychiatric and medical in their origin. Such services tend, at least at the outset, to concentrate upon delinquent, difficult and maladjusted children and to aim at an intensive diagnosis and treatment of a relatively small number of cases. Few of them rest at this, unless other services are already undertaking broader tasks, and many have preventive programmes aimed at the dissemination of knowledge of child development, parent education, collaboration in the training of teachers and so on.

In most countries of Europe, frequently under the inspiration of the Child Guidance Clinics, are to be found *Centres médico-psychologiques, médico-pédagogiques*, or *médico-psycho-pédago-giques* as they are variously called. Many of these operate with the classical team of psychiatrist, psychologist and social worker, some with psychiatrist and social worker only, and are more or less strongly psychiatrically—and often strictly psycho-analytically—oriented. Sometimes they are attached to the out-patient departments of hospitals and, not infrequently, there is no psychologist and they are largely "neuropsychiatric clinics" or "mental health clinics"— with little interest or competence in the educational field. They may have a relatively restricted clientèle, confined to more serious cases and they tend to serve a considerable area rather than to have close functional contacts with local services of various kinds for children. Where circumstances are favourable however—as they were for example in the Child Guidance Clinic at Hill End Hospital, St. Albans, U.K., or the Mental Health services in Amsterdam, Holland—the work undertaken overflows the psychiatric field and, either through collaboration with school psychological and medical services or through direct contact with the schools, devotes some at least, and with the most highly developed services, much of its time to preventive as well as diagnostic and therapeutic work.

In many countries, such clinics have been set up, out of private funds, by University Departments of Medicine, Psychology or Education, by Education Authorities, by Health Authorities or by Hospitals. In some countries—in France for example—the *Centres médico-psychologiques* depend upon a semi-voluntary body itself subventioned by the State and at the same time receive payments upon a case basis from Ministries of Health, Welfare or Education according to circumstances. In others, conventional Child Guidance Clinics exist side by side with School Psychological Services where these are organized; and the fact that each may depend upon a different administrative authority and be financed from a different budget does not necessarily lead either to a duplication of services or to a lack of functional relationship.

There is no need here to describe the aims and function of the typical Child Guidance Clinic with its threefold team, usually psychiatrically directed and adapted peculiarly to the diagnosis and treatment of severely maladjusted, neurotic and psychotic children. Many such descriptions exist.[1] Europe however has seen some interesting and significant developments which, by adaptation to local circumstances and needs have, in spite of administrative and financial limitations, succeeded in providing a wider service. One such is the *Centre psychopédagogique Claude Bernard* described on page 61.

One of the pioneers of the formula in Europe, and a more ambitious and wider spreading example is that begun by Dr. André Répond in 1930 in the Canton of Valais, Switzerland.[2]

PROBLEMS

These few examples indicate the variety of inspiration and objective which underlies European developments in the general

1.   E.g. Burbury, W. M., Balint, E. M. and Yapp, B. J. *An introduction to Child Guidance*, MacMillan, London, 1945. Stevenson, C. & G. Smith, *Child Guidance Clinics: A Quarter Century of Development*, New York, Commonwealth Fund, 1934 and the works by Witmer & Moody previously cited.
2.   Described on pp. 76–77.

field of guidance. The picture is somewhat obscure because almost nowhere has finance and staff been forthcoming to develop all aspects of any service, educational or medical, as seen by its creators. Thus many services which would like to emphasize their preventive rôle have been pressed into a kind of first-aid activity and are obliged to concentrate upon diagnosis and the treatment of a relatively small number of cases; whilst others recognizing the need for constructive work through schools and other community services have not had the funds or skilled personnel necessary to undertake the long-term research, the training and the propaganda which seem to be essential. Only too often, no matter what the point of departure, guidance organizations by the sheer weight of need in comparison with resources are thrust back into a task of a short-term though pressing kind and are unable to develop the longer-term aspects of what they conceive to be their main purpose.

Another great problem—perhaps the key to the whole matter—is that of finding suitable, and suitably trained, staff. Many of the partial realisations owe their one-sidedness as much to the limitations of the training of those who run them as to other factors. The skills and insights of the educational psychologist,—who, it is now coming to be agreed, must have both educational and psychological training and experience—demand a lengthy, carefully contrived and intensive training. There are relatively few centres in Europe where such a training may be obtained. Although many universities offer the necessary basic courses in psychology and education, few indeed as yet have been able to develop the post-graduate, practical and theoretical training through experience in an actual service which is clearly necessary. Moreover, the combination of University studies, of teaching experience and of subsequent training and work under supervision, is one which puts a great financial burden on the student. Many women and more men hesitate to undertake such a training in countries where vocational outlets for psychologists may be limited to some kind of auxiliary status or be rendered insecure because no legal or administrative recognition has yet been granted to their profession. Child psychiatry too is a very recent development of psychiatry and medicine, and possibilities of training in Europe are similarly limited. So far the specialized teachers, social workers, play therapists, psycho-therapists, speech re-educators and the like necessary to a full service can be recruited only ad hoc from among those who shew interest and pick up a training here and there largely by their own talents and industry. Although almost everywhere some kind or kinds of services are beginning or extending their work, in fact the day of the brilliant amateur is by no means over.

Nevertheless for the educational psychologist, centres of training do exist and standards of qualification are growing up in Europe. It is now generally agreed, though by no means enforced without exception, that as well as a sound university training in psychology, the psychologist who is to work in contact with the schools should himself have had considerable experience of teaching. In the United Kingdom, the Committee of Professional Psychologists insists upon an honours degree in psychology, teacher training and at least one year's teaching or other equivalent experience with children and young people. It insists too upon a minimum age of twenty-five before the intending educational psychologist undertakes his one year course of practical training, and withholds recognition until the trainee has successfully passed a further year working under a more experienced psychologist in a service. There are of course exceptions made to this rule; moreover the standards adopted are recommendations only, and local education authorities and other bodies sometimes make appointments of those who do not have such minimum qualifications. On the other hand, University training centres, such as that at University College, London or at the University of Birmingham, often set their standards higher and may require, in particular, a longer experience of teaching.[1] In the Scottish Universities intending educational psychologists are drawn from the ranks of expe-

1.   There are at present five recognized training centres for Educational Psychologists in England providing between them about 18 places for the one year practical post-graduate training.

rienced teachers who pursue studies at the post-graduate level
for the degree of B. Ed.

In France, school psychologists are recruited from the ranks
of primary and secondary teachers who have had at least five
years of successful full-time teaching experience. They pursue
a course spread over two years in the *Institut de Psychologie* of
the University of Paris leading at least to the Diploma in
Educational Psychology (*Diplôme de psycho-pédagogie*) and in
most cases to the Diploma in Applied Psychology as well
(*Diplôme de psychologie appliquée*). Many have in addition
other diplomas—as teachers of backward children, vocational
guidance officers and the like.

Elsewhere in Europe (e.g. Austria, Denmark, Norway) similar
standards of qualification and training are becoming established.
University Centres such as the *Institut des Sciences de l'Education*
(University of Geneva), the Departments of Education and
Psychology at the University of Utrecht, the Department of
Psychology of the Free University of Berlin have set up services
of demonstration and research in which the practical training
of educational psychologists may be undertaken concurrently
with theoretical studies. So too institutions exist, under the
State or under Universities—such for example as the Erica
Institute in Sweden[1]—for the training of such specialised staff
as play-therapists; and others, in most countries, to train teachers
for handicapped, maladjusted, subnormal, retarded and other
categories of children as well as to conduct courses for teachers
interested in the general problems of the guidance of normal
children and the identification of those for whom some form of
special education or remedial treatment is necessary.

1. A recent Swedish report on the training of psychologists is referred
to on pp. 73–74.

PART II

THE SITUATION IN SOME EUROPEAN COUNTRIES

Many of the types of service and many of the trends of development so far discussed exist side by side in the various countries of Europe. Almost nowhere are services as fully developed as those well acquainted with the problems would wish and in few do they cover the whole country. The picture is one of experimentation and of fluctuation.

Some of this is due to the difficulty of estimating needs, and of bringing into relation with a service, all those individuals and organizations which have something to contribute; partly it is because needs and problems which have existed for years do not make themselves overtly felt until a new service has demonstrated its utility and won the confidence of teachers and parents. A common experience is for a small service rapidly to be overwhelmed with demands for assistance the moment it becomes known, and to be left with very little time or staff available for the necessary preventive and constructive tasks which alone will in the long run diminish the load of cases for diagnosis and treatment. Conversely where the level of teacher training is high and where a service can collaborate in the training of specialised social workers, remedial teachers, educational and vocational guidance officers, many of the tasks which it may have to assume initially, can later be delegated effectively, allowing the psychological staff to fall into a consultative, coordinating and research rôle except for those cases requiring expert attention.

The essential nature of a good psychological service is its adaptability and sensitivity to needs; and it is just this that does not shew in official reports or in research papers; nor would an elaborate tabulation of case loads, staffing or other administrative data provide the answer. The following descriptions therefore of the services in certain countries must be regarded as illustrative of existing initiatives and concepts rather than as a series of evaluative studies.

Austria[1]

In a great many ways, Austria presents the picture of a country where psychological services have a considerable history and where, since the end of the last war, educational reform has been accompanied by an extension and systematization of guidance services. Those concerned with the welfare of children have steadily become more and more aware of the complexity of the problems which have to be faced and solved. The classical fields of behaviour difficulty, emotional and intellectual abnormality, delinquency and the like continue of course to attract attention and help. Increased emphasis however is being put on various more subtle and less spectacular aspects of preventive and remedial work. In recent articles in the official publication of the Ministry of Education (*Pädagogische Mitteilungen*), attention is drawn to the needs for educational and vocational guidance, to the problems of general and specific retardation, backwardness and school failure, to the need for research into the age at which children should begin school, and into the difficulties which may be experienced by children transferred from one class or school to another.

Similarly a great effort has been made to increase the facilities for special educational treatment. The number of specialised teachers was estimated at some 800 in 1952—double the number that existed in 1945. Nearly 500 special classes for rather more than 8,000 subnormal children, six schools for some seven hundred deaf, eighty five special classes for 1,500 maladjusted children, four institutions for the blind, thirteen classes for partially sighted, and eleven for speech defectives, are now established and represent a considerable provision for exceptional children. Only the needs of the physically handicapped (47 classes for 791 children) seem not to be adequately met and it is estimated that some 200 such children do not receive the necessary special educational help.[2] The school psychological

1. Based upon the very full information provided by the Austrian National Commission for Unesco.
2. Führing, M., "Der Ausbau des Sonderschulwesens". *Pädagogische Mitteilungen*, Jahrg. 1952. Stück 11.

services, as well as other guidance organizations, have close connections with special schools in their area. In one province (Salzburg) special guidance services exist for the deaf and for the mentally subnormal.[1]

Since 1922 the provision of an adequate form of cumulative school record card for use by teachers, the school medical service, and the services of educational and vocational guidance, has been recognized as a basic step. Immediately after the war the experimental forms used before the war in a few schools were modified and improved, and in 1949-50 the system was introduced into all State Schools and made compulsory by ministerial decree.[2] This record form which systematises social, educational, physical and psychological data on each child, depends for its effectiveness upon the knowledge and skill particularly of the teachers. Hence it has been made the subject of short courses for teachers and the Ministry of Education has issued a detailed handbook to accompany it.

It is on this basis of growing preoccupation with all forms of guidance that school psychological services proper have developed in the postwar period in the capital and in some of the provinces (Oberösterreich, Tirol and Steiermark).

In a report made in 1947-48[3] the Federal Ministry of Education estimated that some 750 specially trained[4] teachers were employed on psychological work, in the ratio of one to 150-400 pupils between the age of 10 and 14. Their task was that of examining each pupil in these age groups once a year as the basis of educational and vocational guidance and of examining other pupils as necessary. Since then, cautiously, the services

1. Asperger, H., "Schulpsychologischer Dienst in Österreich". *Pädagogische Mitteilungen*, Jahrg. 1952, Stück 11.
2. Decree No. 16285 IV/15/49. June 15, 1949. See Lang, L., *Neue Wege zur Schülerkenntnis*, p. 253, and "Dreissig Jahre Schülerbeschreibung in Österreich". *Pädagogische Mitteilungen*, Jahrg. 1952, Stück 5.
3. XIth International Conference on Public Education, Geneva 1948. *School Psychologists*, Paris, Unesco; Geneva, I.B.E., 1948, p. 42.
4. Having had five years of teaching experience, studied psychology at the University level, and having completed a special course of professional training organized by the Ministry of Education.

have been developed until their type may be illustrated by that of Vienna, directed by Dr. Schenk-Danzinger, and founded in 1948[1] under the auspices of the education authorities. It is staffed by six psychologists, two social workers and a medical consultant and works in five rooms set aside in a school building. Its principal tasks are the discovery, examination and treatment of learning and behaviour difficulties in children, of maladjustments of all kinds, and advice to teachers, schools and the educational administration. The main means of remedy at the disposal of the service are the guidance of a child to a special class or school, aid to the teacher in handling the problem himself, referral of certain cases of marked social or family difficulty to welfare agencies, psychotherapy, remedial education on a part-time basis for children with specific difficulties, and a small continuing class for slow developing children (*Förderklasse*) under a specialized teacher. In addition, the service conducts a weekly consultation for parents in three of its schools.

The important feature of this service is its close connection with the educational system generally including the special schools and classes of the City and its environs. The psychological and educational examination of each child referred is preceded by a detailed report from the teacher and supplemented by a careful family study. When the case study is completed, a report is sent to the teacher and to the school inspector responsible, along with recommendations for further action if required. An idea both of the caseload of the service (apart from and in addition to the more general and preventive work undertaken) and of the way in which demand has grown is given by the fact that in 1948-49, 180 cases were undertaken as compared with 1,280 in the year 1954-55, the large majority referred by the teachers themselves.

Most of the provincial services are not as fully developed and staffed. That however of Upper Austria, directed by Dr.

1. Schenk-Danzinger, L., "Die Schulpsychologische Beratungsstelle des Stadtschulrates für Wien". *Pädagogische Mitteilungen*, Jahrg. 1953, Stück 1.

Sparowitz,[1] has many interesting features. Recognizing that much of the effectiveness of a psychological service depends on the level of understanding, training and cooperativeness of the teachers themselves, the psychological staff assist in the initial training of teachers; and, in 1951-52, they ran a thorough training course in Linz for selected, experienced teachers who become psychological counsellors to their schools and, in cooperation with the psychological service, undertake much of the first line discovery of problems, and remedial education. The service also provides a "parents' school" and, in conjunction with the vocational guidance service, ensures the continuous guidance of children from school entry to the beginning of the working life. It works closely with the special schools and classes which are well developed in Upper Austria. In addition, because perhaps of its markedly eclectic outlook and strongly educational orientation, the staff of the service is engaged in ongoing research into such important problems as school readiness,[2] problems of adaptation to the Middle School, and problems of adjustment to working life.

In Vienna itself, the School Psychological Service is supplemented by the Guidance Service for Grammar Schools (*Beratungsstelle für Mittelschüler*)[3] and by the service of guidance established for the technical schools by the Viennese education authorities in 1951. The first of these centres which works solely in the Grammar Schools (children and adolescents from 10-18 years of age) of the city was established at first as a private initiative[4] in 1950, but now is subventioned by the education and social affairs authorities. Its principal preoccupations are the examination and treatment of difficult pupils referred mainly by the schools themselves. Its research and preventive work is

1. Sparowitz, E., "Der Schulpsychologische Dienst in Oberösterreich". *Pädagogische Mitteilungen*. Jahrg. 1953, Stück 5.
2. For a description of the types of the tests and methods used by some services, see: Holzinger, F., "Schulpsychologische Untersuchungen im Bezirk Fürstenfeld". *Pädagogische Mitteilungen*, Jahrg. 1953, Stück 4.
3. Bolterauer, L., "Die Wiener Beratungsstelle für Mittelschüler". *Pädagogische Mitteilungen*, Jahrg. 1953, Stück 2.
4. *August Aichhorn-Gesellschaft.*

limited and the tasks of advising teachers, of general pupil guidance and the like, do not rank among the major aims, though there is some parent education and guidance through a parents' club. It resembles the conventional child guidance clinic both in its field of operation and in its staffing which consists of a psychiatrist, two psychologists, and two specialized educators who undertake much of the remedial and therapeutic work.

The guidance service for technical schools is directed by a psychologist and has a staff of another psychologist, a social worker and a psychiatric consultant paid for by the Viennese Social Security authorities.

In addition to these in Vienna and in some of the provinces, there are Youth Bureaux (*Jugendämter*) which also undertake guidance, the examination and the treatment of educational and behavioural difficulties.

Such general services of guidance and remedial education and therapy are completed by a country wide service of vocational guidance and information.[1] In 1946, the Ministry of Education set up a Central Bureau of Vocational Guidance (*Referat "Schule und Beruf"*), and followed this by establishing in each region a vocational guidance officer or service (*Landesreferent für "Schule und Beruf"*). The central office issues a series of pamphlets giving detailed information on jobs and professions, the conditions and possibilities of training and the like, copies of which go to every school in the country. The tasks of the regional officers are vocational guidance and preparation for the choice of work, the necessary educational and psychological guidance which may be the preliminary to this, and the training of teachers who in one way or another may be involved. The vocational guidance officers are usually themselves experienced teachers who have attended training courses organized by the Ministry. For the more specialized psychological work and especially where individual psychological examination is necessary, they are assisted by fully trained psychologists. In at least one province (Steiermark) a travelling service which will

1. Timp, O., "Das Referat "Schule und Beruf" im Bundesministerium für Unterricht". *Pädagogische Mitteilungen*, Jahrg. 1952, Stück 12.

include remedial education and direct psychological advice to the schools is proposed. Vocational placement and guidance after the educational period, is dealt with by the Ministry of Social Affairs (*Bundesministerium für soziale Verwaltung*) through its Labour Exchanges and Placement Officers. Considerable stress is laid upon the fullest co-operation between the school psychological services, the vocational guidance services, the placement services of the Social Affairs Ministry and the Youth Bureau (*Jugendamt*).

In the capital and in most of the provinces, services of the types described above exist, either singly or together, more or less thinly spread according to their state of development and to needs. In addition, in certain places, there are clinics, centres and travelling services provided by universities, by hospitals, or by private institutions. Many of these are highly developed and provide a comprehensive system of advice, guidance, psychological examination, therapy and remedial education. For example, in the province of Kärnten where no school psychological service exists, the work of the Youth Bureau and of the Vocational Guidance service is completed by the Neurological, Remedial Education and Educational Guidance service (*Nervenambulatorium und Heilpädagogische Beratungsstelle*). This organization has an observation centre and a travelling service which ensures regular examinations in all the schools of the province. In addition, it undertakes the in-training of teachers and social workers, laying special emphasis on remedial education.[1] In Salzburg (town and province) it is the Institute of Comparative Education which assures the psychological service (*Erziehungsberatungsstelle am Institut für vergleichende Erziehungswissenschaft*). In the Tyrol, as well as the schools psychological service, the Innsbruck Neurological Clinic (*Kinderstation der Nervenklinik*, Innsbruck) provides a service of psychiatric and educational diagnosis and guidance, and the Psychotherapeutic Institute undertakes guidance and therapy for children, adolescents and adults. In Vienna itself the University Pediatric Clinic has a Remedial Education Centre (*Heil-*

1.   Asperger, H. Loc. cit. pp. 99/100.

pädagogische Abteilung der Universitäts-Kinderklinik) with a case load of some 3,000 each year for rapid diagnosis and three hundred under observation and treatment, whilst the Psychiatric Clinic has started a general psychiatric service for children and another for epileptics. In addition there is the *Institut für Erziehungshilfe*, run on Adlerian principles and similar in conception to the conventional Child Guidance Clinic, which includes parent guidance among its more usual activities.

Educational thought in Austria is tending more and more to emphasize that the principal responsibility for the guidance of school children and their parents, for making of education a global and constructive process, rests upon the individual teacher, aided, it is true, by the psychological specialist and by such devices as the cumulative school record. Hence while psychology is being brought more and more into direct relationship with education and educational method and while a considerable further development of school psychological services may be expected, a major effort is being directed to the training of the teachers themselves in understanding children and their developmental problems.

BELGIUM[1]

Belgium was early a pioneer of vocational guidance and of the psychometric methods which underlay its development in the early part of this century. Similarly the applications of child study to the improvement of education, at first through the work of pioneers like Decroly, and later in the ordinary work of the schools, have had a considerable history. It is not surprising therefore that one of the first school psychological services in Europe, the "*Laboratoire de pédagogie et de psychologie de l'enfant*", should have been set up in 1928 at Angleur,[2] for five

1. The information given here is based largely upon an article by Prof. F. Hotyat "La psychologie scolaire en Belgique", *Enfance*, Vol. 8. No. I. 1955.

2. For a full description see Jadoulle, A. *Le Laboratoire pédagogique au travail*. Paris, Editions du Scarabée, 1951.

primary schools in an industrial suburb of Liège. Its particular tasks were defined with great foresight. Under the direction of an educational psychologist, it conducts systematic surveys of the school population (physical and mental status, educational methods and material used), undertakes research in the improvement of education, especially through the supervision of experimental classes, and, in conjunction with the school medical service, ensures the sound development of all children. In addition it makes a special individual psychological study —and, if necessary, undertakes the remedial education—of all children who are difficult, refractory, failing in their work or absent from school for more than a fortnight. All children beginning school are examined with group and individual tests, and for each a record is prepared which brings together the psychological information along with medical, social and other data cumulatively gathered during the child's school career. On this basis, and on that of subsequent examinations, the staff of the Laboratoire aid parents and teachers in the guidance of children, especially towards the end of the primary school period. Through its experimental class and in other ways, the service contributes to the practical training of teachers in the new educational methods with which it is experimenting or has developed.

A rather similar service is that set up on a voluntary basis by the *Ecole Normale Charles Buls* in Brussels for the 800 pupils of five schools. The basis of the work done is the individual cumulative record for each child which contains medical, social, psychological and educational data. From 1945 to 1951 the service developed a number of specialised sections—such as medical gymnastics, a holiday home in the country, research activities concerned with the interaction of emotional and educational factors in personality disturbance, psychological guidance and a special educational service for subnormal children.

Since the war a number of larger communes have instituted services—like those of Liège and Forest-les-Bruxelles (1947) —covering primary and secondary schools. The work undertaken is less intensive than that of Angleur or the Ecole Normale Charles Buls, largely because each centre deals with a school population of several thousand. It consists mainly in the group testing of pupils at first entry to primary and secondary school, and at school leaving; and, at the request of parents, more detailed psychological examination of individual children for educational or vocational guidance and, in some cases, of children with difficulties of social or educational adaptation.

Certain large technical schools have organized their own guidance services. That of the Université du Travail at Charleroi, for example, conducts entrance tests for the selection of students, works with the teaching staff in the progressive vocational guidance of pupils, and helps to standardise the examinations used by the school. Individual cases of failure are examined and the service has at its disposal services of remedial gymnastics, and social welfare as well as holiday homes.

In 1947, as an experiment, the Ministry of Education set up a number of *centres psychomédicosociaux*, and at present, there are fifteen such centres in the country. In general, these are set up inside a Lycée or Athénée and serve a school population of boys and girls in primary and secondary classes varying in number between 1,500 and 4,500 pupils. In general there is a psychologist responsible to the head of the school, assisted by a social worker and by the school medical officer; sometimes, in addition, there is a junior psychologist to conduct and score group tests. The principal emphasis of these services is upon progressive educational and vocational guidance and upon day to day collaboration with the teaching staff in the solution of the problems and difficulties of individual children, as well as upon cooperative research in educational method.

As in other countries, numerous services directly and indirectly concerned with the psychological care of children exist outside the educational system and a certain number of publicly or privately financed clinics of the child guidance type have been set up under hospital or university auspices and by religious bodies. In certain cases, these have realised a close functional and administrative liaison with the educational services. A striking example is that of the *Dispensaire d'Hygiène Mentale* at La Louvière which has integrated its activity into the educational system of the commune and works closely with the administrative authorities, the school inspectors and the teachers. Among other achievements, this combined service instituted a system of standardised examinations at the end of each school year on the basis of which those children who are weakest educationally are screened out for careful individual study. According to their mental level they are then guided to B or C classes the function of which is an education designed so far as possible to remedy their weakness. In addition a class has been set up for the subnormal, and a short term hostel for those who need to be reeducated away from their family is projected.

DENMARK[1]

Since 1924 a Commission for Educational Psychological Research has existed in Denmark, consisting of representatives of teachers' organisations, pedagogical associations and research psychologists. With limited financial means, this Commission carried out invaluable work in the field of educational psychology and pedagogics, until it was superseded recently by the Danish Pedagogical Institute founded by the State and led by three psychologists.

Psychological services began to develop actively in the mid 1930's, when work was commenced by the municipal authorities in Copenhagen. Since then developments have been gradual and sure, and at the time of writing, nearly all Denmark is covered by some form of school psychological service. The nature of these is illustrated by that which serves Frederiksberg, a sector of Copenhagen, and an urban municipality of some 115,000 inhabitants, with 12,000 children in the 13 municipal schools. Under the aegis of the educational authorities, there

1. The information on which this account is based has been provided by Prof. E. Tranekjær Rasmussen, Mr. H. C. Rasmussen (School Psychologist), and Mr. Harald Torpe head of the school psychological office at Frederiksberg.

is a school psychological office in the town hall, staffed by
10 psychologists, all of whom possess a university qualification
in psychology.

This office is primarily diagnostic and advisory in function
and its work is based on collaboration with the school and the
home. Referrals are voluntary, although the past years have seen
a steady increase in the amount of work, and have shown that
the advice tendered by the educational psychologists as to the
treatment and instruction of the children is nearly always
followed. An idea of the scope of the service is given by the fact
that about 500 new cases are investigated each year, which
means that some 20-22 % of the pupils attending the public
schools in the municipality come into contact with the office
at some time.

If a pupil finds it difficult to maintain his place in his class
or has any other difficulty of adjustment, his teacher may refer
him, with the consent of his parents, to the school psychological
office. The teacher completes a report form, describing the
child's educational level, general behaviour, etc. The school
physician in turn informs the office as to the child's physical
development, vision, hearing, etc. The parents are then invited
to the office with their child. The psychologist first discusses the
problem with the parents in an attempt to elucidate the domestic
background for the child's difficulties. A case study of the child
himself is then undertaken by means of tests and interview,
sometimes within a period of one or two hours, and sometimes
through a series of sessions spread over several days.

The usual types of tests are employed, such as the common
performance tests (Healy Picture Completion, form-boards,
etc.) and the Danish revision of the Binet-Simon scale. In
addition, standardised attainment, projective and personality
tests are used whenever necessary.[1]

1. The projective tests may be purchased at any bookshop in Denmark.
The Danish revision of the Binet-Simon as well as a series of attainment
tests standardised by the Commission for Educational Psychological
research are restricted in their sale either to qualified psychologists or, as
far as the attainment tests are concerned, to teachers. The materials and

When the study of the child and his circumstances has been completed, the matter is discussed with the parents and with the school, and a written report including the results of the study of the child and the conclusions based upon it is forwarded to the teachers. The interest and cooperation of the parents is indicated by the fact that a quarter of the cases referred to the Frederiksberg office in 1954-55 came on the initiative of the parents themselves. Sometimes it is possible to solve the problem simply by means of parent counselling and advice to the school. Should the child however prove to be mildly mentally subnormal or backward, he may be transferred to a "special aid" school, on the recommendation of his teacher and the head of the receiving school, and, if necessary, without the consent of his parents. Pupils in such schools usually have an I.Q. of between 70 and 90, and total roughly 1.5 % of the municipality's children of compulsory school age. In other municipalities, the figure sometimes reaches 3 %. There are never more than 15 children in a class in the special aid schools. Stress is laid on individual instruction, and special teaching materials have been devised, with financial support from the State. The teachers in charge have at least training as primary school teachers, and most have completed further special courses. Moderately and severely sub-normal children (with I.Q. under 70) do not attend these schools but are usually reported to a special board, which then removes the children from the normal school organisation and places them either in a residential institution or, as is becoming more usual, in a special day school.

A far larger group of cases is composed of pupils with reading and spelling difficulties. In Frederiksberg, almost 6 % of the children of compulsory school age and of normal or super-normal ability receive some form of special instruction. In very serious cases, this may be given in a reading class, where there are never more than 16 children, under a specially trained teacher. Where the difficulties are less pronounced, an attempt is made to keep the child in his ordinary class, and special

other documents for internal use, are published by a firm established by the Danish psychologists for their own purposes.

reading tuition is provided for 15 minutes daily, in private, at school, during school hours. The educational psychologist follows the pupil's development by means of regular control tests, and together with the teacher decides when ordinary school work may be recommenced. Special tuition in arithmetic is only rarely provided.

The provision for maladjusted children is more difficult to describe since maladjustment may cover many different things, and the advice that can be given and the procedures adopted will naturally vary considerably. Where the main problem is conflict between the child and its school or between home and school, transfer to another class or school is sometimes recommended. More recently there has been a tendency for the educational psychologists to add to their normal diagnostic and advisory tasks a limited amount of remedial work, especially play therapy. This can, of course, only be carried out with the full cooperation of the home and school.

Frederiksberg municipality also has a special residential school open all the year round where difficult boys may be placed for shorter or longer periods, and where the principal means of treatment is a radical change in environment. Such residential schools may prove excellent for children whose difficulties arise mainly from their home circumstances and many improve considerably after a period in one of them, where they are free, and treated with understanding and friendliness. But as most difficult children come from environments which have at least contributed to their difficulties, problems arise again when they return home. Hence the educational psychologist concerned, in conjunction with the head of the school (himself a trained psychologist), undertakes the re-education of the parents so that they adopt a positive attitude towards the child, an essential if the child's return is to be a success. Sometimes conditions are so difficult, that it is necessary to remove the child permanently from his home; but this is a matter for the child welfare authorities. The Central Copenhagen municipality has several such schools for girls and boys, as well as a number of observation classes. The latter are of two types: those concerned with difficult children, and those for children who, in spite of normal or supernormal intelligence, are failing in one or more school subjects.

Prior to sending a child to an observation centre or residential school, and sometimes even before play therapy is commenced, the psychological office asks for a psychiatric consultation. Normally the waiting list for diagnosis and advice is not long, but if some form of therapy is decided upon, the child may have to wait a long time, and many cases that really ought to receive treatment must be disregarded. A few cases may be referred to Copenhagen University Child Guidance Clinic, but the waiting list here is full for a year ahead. This clinic, directed by a psychologist, has a staff comprising psychologists, social workers, a psychiatrist and a pediatrician. The clinic, established originally with aid from the Rockefeller Foundation and now maintained by the State, carries out scientific as well as clinical work, and trains psychologists, who have graduated from the university, in child therapy.

Cases demanding psychiatric treatment are referred to the child psychiatric departments of the Copenhagen municipal hospitals or to the University hospital. Here again the waiting lists are long, and the places available too few to satisfy present needs.

Another feature of the Frederiksberg psychological service is that one of its psychologists is attached to the infant welfare centre, where parents may bring their children for medical examination between the ages of 1 and 7 years. If the physician considers it necessary, or if the parents so wish, they are referred for interview to the psychologist. He may in turn refer them to the school psychological office for a full study. Similarly the office cooperates with private medical practioners, institutes for the "word-blind", etc. and with the municipal child welfare board over cases referred by the board, or in supplying information concerning children who have been examined, and later for some reason are reported to the board.

The office also carries out tests for determining educational maturity. Hitherto these have most frequently been individual, since no suitable group tests are available in Denmark. However the office is at present conducting experiments in the hope of developing an adequate group test. A certain amount of public education in educational and psychological matters, particularly as concerns special educational provision is also undertaken. The psychologists take part too in courses for teachers arranged by the educational authorities and in meetings of parents held at the individual schools.

The aims and organization of the service in Frederiksberg are with certain modifications similar to other school psychological offices in Denmark. Many of those in the larger towns, however, are either completely unable to undertake play therapy, or can only do so to a very restricted extent, and there are only a few observation centres. In some towns, school readiness tests are more generally applied than is the case in Frederiksberg, and in one town there are kindergarten classes which function as a transition between kindergarten and school. The school psychological office of the municipality of Central Copenhagen, the largest in Denmark, caters for a school population of 97,000 pupils and employs 26 university-trained psychologists, some of whom are only part-time, which is equivalent to a full-time staff of twenty psychologists.

School psychological work in country districts presents greater difficulties. There is still even in the market towns a considerable need for the extension of services, but there are good reasons to suppose that this need will eventually be satisfied. At present each county has at least a consultant in special education, who may be called upon by the teachers for advice as to how they may best cater for the various categories of pupils within the limits set by the facilities available at the school concerned. The consultants test the children and demonstrate various types of teaching materials. About half the consultants have a university training in psychology, the remainder being elementary school teachers who have received more or less extensive supplementary training. The lack of uniformity in this respect is unsatisfactory. Professional opinion holds that consultants without a full university training do not have the requisite background to enable them to carry out the testing connected with their work, and they cannot administer personality tests. It is to be expected that all such consultantships will in time be filled by fully trained psychologists.

Normally the psychological offices do not concern themselves with psychotechnical investigations nor with vocational guidance, except in a few cases in connection with children already attending for other reasons. Parents who desire vocational guidance for their children go to the central employment bureau, if they are resident in Greater Copenhagen. A psychological investigation may then be recommended, which is carried out at the Copenhagen Municipal Psychotechnical Institute. This latter has a university-trained psychologist as its chief, and there are several trained psychologists on its staff. Vocational counsellors are often teachers. An Act has recently been passed to ensure that all Danish children may receive vocational guidance, and is being put into practice at the time of writing.

The school psychological offices in the larger municipalities are on the whole large enough not to need any considerable extension in order to carry out current research projects in addition to their ordinary advisory functions. Such research as has been undertaken so far has however usually been confined to enquiries suggested by the schools themselves; thus reading problems have been well studied, but not those one meets in arithmetic. Moreover whilst the work of diagnosis and advice has gradually been extended within the framework of the public elementary schools, the senior secondary schools and private schools, attended by a relatively small proportion of children, have not to any great extent been drawn into it. Similarly much more time could be profitably devoted to treatment, particularly as the need for this appears to be increasing.

The only recognised training for psychological work in Denmark is that given at the University of Copenhagen. Just after the war, courses were commenced with the specific aim of preparing school psychologists. Until then, the degree in psychology was mainly directed to a preparation for research work. This older degree was retained, while the new degree of

Candidatus Psychologiae was designed for more practical work and much of the strictly professional training is provided after the degree has been obtained. The main subjects covered by the degree are: general psychology, child psychology, and the psychology of the various school subjects, as well as their pathology. So far some 250 students have obtained the degree of candidatus psychologiae of whom approximately 80 are concerned with work in the schools. Since an increasing proportion of those who qualify go on, not to work with the schools but to clinical work, work with delinquents, to child welfare posts and to employment in the armed services, the course of study no longer fully satisfies all current needs. The curriculum therefore will soon be revised, to include among other things, a certain number of optional specialisations and some practical professional training prior to the degree. The length of the course will then become a minimum of 5 years.

At present, those who wish to be clinical psychologists receive their practical training after graduation at hospital clinics or at the University Child Guidance Clinic. The Danish Psychological Association also to some extent aids its members in their further training by means of special courses, for example in the use of the Rorschach test, and by shorter courses of a more general nature.

Prior to studying psychology all educational psychologists have completed a training as elementary school teachers and have had at least five years of practical teaching experience. Furthermore as part of their professional duties and to ensure a real and continuing contact with the work of the schools, they are required to teach twelve hours a week in an elementary school, with the exception of senior psychologists who may teach only six hours. Salaries are comparable to those of teachers, senior psychologists being paid as headmasters of schools and assistant psychologists as assistant heads of schools.

The Scandinavian psychological associations cooperate with each other, and hold an inter-Scandinavian congress every third year, as well as publishing a joint Scandinavian psychological journal.

FRANCE

In France the science of child psychology has a long history though its full application to the day to day problems of the schools is relatively recent, and by no means complete. Mainly as a result of the work of Binet and Simon, each area has a medico-educational commission (*Commission médico-pédagogique*) which consists of medical specialists, teachers specialised in the education of the subnormal and, where they are available, of psychologists. These commissions have the specific task of finding those children who cannot follow the normal courses in the primary schools—usually the mentally subnormal or educationally retarded. In addition there are the social workers who, among their many tasks, have that of the detection of abnormal family conditions, of aiding where they can and of referring the more serious cases to specialised services. Under the Ministries of Education, Health and Justice, as well as under private auspices are organized various services of special schools and classes for blind, deaf, partially sighted, hard of hearing, delicate, physically handicapped, mentally subnormal, maladjusted, delinquent and homeless[1] children. For example, for mentally subnormal children (i.e. between I.Q. 60 — I.Q. 87) there are some 1,300 special day classes[2] annexed to ordinary schools or independently constituted, with a total attendance of about 20,000. One thousand feeble minded children are catered for in day centres which combine educational or vocational training with medical care, and a further 10,000 are cared for in residential custodial establishments and psychiatric hospitals, and 7,000 in *Centres médico-pédagogiques* or residential schools.[3] Provision on a similar scale exists for other officially recognized

1.   The *Association Nationale des Communautés d'Enfants* which receives a subvention from the Ministry of Education groups over two hundred residential institutions for children, of all types, financed either by the various ministries directly, indirectly subventioned on a case basis by the ministries, by the *Assurances Sociales*, or maintained by voluntary agencies or individual groups.

2.   *Classes ou écoles de perfectionnement annexes ou autonomes.*

3.   Report by the French Child Welfare Organizations to the International Child Welfare Congress, Zagreb, 1954.

groups; and in one or two places attempts have been made to develop special opportunities for the highly gifted and for intelligent maladjusted children. The Ministry of Education has also instituted full time (six months) training courses for teachers, already experienced in ordinary schools, who wish to specialise in the teaching of physically handicapped or mentally subnormal children.

The *classes nouvelles*[1] represent a considerable effort in another direction, that of the improvement of education and educational method by making it more child-centred, more active, and with more emphasis upon a thorough psycho-social and educational study of the pupil. All of these classes officially have been situated in the secondary schools under the care of specially trained teachers who volunteered for the task; but similar experiments have been tried in primary schools; and in a few cases whole schools, primary and secondary, devote themselves entirely to pilot projects in the newer methods, often in close association with psychological services or research institutions of various kinds.[2] One of the most important aspects of the classes nouvelles from the present viewpoint is their experimental use of a cumulative school record card for each pupil which in addition to medical and social data contains a considerable section devoted to a continuous study and recording of the child's educational and psychological development, where possible by means of standardized educational and psychological tests as well as by systematised observations. This is made the basis of careful educational and subsequently vocational guidance giving reality and substance to the corresponding organization of the six years of secondary studies into a *"cycle d'orientation"* (the first three years) and a *"cycle de détermination"* (the second three years).

1. Now called *"Classes pilotes"*.
2. The Lycée de Sèvres which forms part of the Centre International d'études pédagogiques de Sèvres, and the Ecole Nouvelle de Boulogne-sur-Seine which works in close cooperation with the Centre d'Entraînement aux Méthodes Actives, and the Centre Psycho-pédagogique du Lycée Claude Bernard, Paris.

It is against this background of partial but progressive and experimental educational reform, that the special services must be viewed. As in other countries, these services are incomplete, financed from different ministries and relatively unintegrated on a national level, though, locally, official and ad hoc collaboration between them ensures as full a coverage as possible. As elsewhere, too, informed opinion considers the existing services inadequate to meet the real needs and there are marked divergencies from place to place in the capacity of local services to meet all the demands made upon them.

The only service which is fully organized throughout France is that of vocational guidance for those children who leave school for work at the end of the period of compulsory schooling. In every department there is at least one vocational guidance service staffed by an officer who has been trained essentially in psychometric methods. A projected reform suggests that the training of these staff should be widened so that they may extend their field of operation beyond the immediate task of vocational testing and the giving of information on jobs.

Complementary to this service is the *"Service d'Orientation scolaire et universitaire"* (Service of School and University Guidance) organized by the Bureau Universitaire de Statistique (University Bureau of Statistics), a public service provided by the Ministry of Education. This service was founded in 1937 originally as a research project to devise methods of psychological investigation suitable for the academic secondary schools, and for the Universities and higher education generally; but it rapidly developed into a full service of guidance for the secondary schools, the Universities and the institutions of University status.

A study is made of all pupils entering the first year of their secondary course in the cooperating schools. This *"dossier scolaire"* is based upon a report made by the child's teachers in the previous classes, a questionnaire addressed to the families, a questionnaire completed by the pupils themselves, a series of standardized group tests of attainment, capacity and personality and is completed by an analysis of the cause of deficiencies and a psychological analysis of all the data. Where it seems justified, where the school requests it, or at the wish of a parent, the service undertakes individual examinations as a result of which it may advise parents or the school, suggest a more detailed medical or psychological examination or recommend a change of course or school in the hope of finding something better adapted to the child's tastes and capacities. A similar service is offered not only throughout the six or more years of the secondary academic course but also for the guidance of intending University students or those who, having begun a course of study, wish for help or to make a change.

The service is staffed mainly by psychologists who hold both the Diploma of Vocational Guidance (*Diplôme d'orientation professionnelle*, a state diploma) and the diploma of educational psychology and of applied psychology (*Diplômes de psychopédagogie et de psychologie appliquée*, awarded by the Institut de Psychologie, University of Paris); but has as consultants specialist teachers in the Lycées and Universities, and medical specialists of various kinds. It does not undertake remedial work or therapy but works in liaison with school medical and psychological services, vocational guidance services and psychiatric departments of hospitals or clinics to which it sends appropriate cases. In conjunction with its parent organization, the University Statistical Bureau, it undertakes a considerable body of research work concentrated mainly upon the classes preparing pupils for higher technical education, and university entrance, and upon the factors making for vocational success or failure in the liberal professions.

In contrast to this service, in France, as elsewhere in Europe, there exists a great number of services of varying structure, finance and objectives engaged mainly in the diagnosis and treatment of educationally, socially and emotionally maladjusted children and of delinquents. Some of these are privately financed and managed, others are of a public or semi-public nature, most receive state aid in one form or another, either through subventions or on the basis of payments from the Social Insurance, Public Assistance, the Ministry of Health or the Ministry of Education on a case basis. Most of these organizations in France are members of regional branches of *l'Union Nationale des Associations régionales pour la Sauvegarde de l'Enfance et de l'Adolescence*, a group of bodies recognized and financed by the State, which organizes technical conferences, sponsors local initiatives, and publishes a journal carrying research and other papers written by its members.

A considerable proportion of these services are psychiatric and medical in their direction—Consultations, Bureaux, Dispensaires d'Hygiène Mentale, Neuropsychiatric Clinics, Centres Medico-Psychologiques—and are concerned mainly with the examination of subnormal children, and the discovery and diagnosis of maladjustment. Many of them have only a psychiatrist and social worker as their staff, though some have a psychologist, a specialised teacher, lay psychotherapists, speech reeducators and others as well. Largely because of staffing difficulties, rather fewer than half undertake remedial work, psychotherapy, or the more general educative and preventive tasks of informing teachers, parents and others, and the conduct of research work. In some cases the psychological and psychiatric work is directly integrated with the school health service; in others with the public health service; in some cases a service operates from a University or a hospital clinic; in others it takes the form of a child guidance clinic working outside the educational system but serving school children and their parents over a considerable area. Apart from official services, or services provided by lay bodies, there are those financed by religious and especially Catholic groups.

In a number of regions, religious bodies, private societies, and official bodies, some affiliated to the *Association pour la Sauvegarde de l'Enfance et de l'Adolescence*, run observation centres. As their name suggests, these are centres which board children for a short or long period during which a diagnosis of difficulties may be made on the basis of their behaviour; they tend however more and more to combine with this the function of short-term remedial and therapeutic institutions rather like residential schools for maladjusted children. Similarly there are reeducation centres whose primary purpose is that of helping retarded and maladjusted children but which also take on some diagnostic functions. In general the case loads of these Observation Centres are between 100 and 150 children yearly, the number tending to decrease in proportion as the Centre undertakes treatment. The *Consultations d'hygiène mentale*, the *Centres médico-psychologiques* and similar services—many of which are not full-time—tend to have annual case loads of between 100 and 200 new cases for diagnosis, though some are much above this figure. It seems also that the Observation Centres receive the majority of their cases from the courts, the *Consultations d'hygiène mentale*, and the Social Services, whereas, for the other types of service which do not provide boarding accomodation, the source of referral in something like a third of their cases is the social services while another quarter come from the schools. Referrals from the school health services, and from private medical practitioners are relatively few.[1]

Among the more interesting initiatives of the *Sauvegarde de l'Enfance* to bring psychology and psychiatry more fully and closely into relation with the life of the school and through this, with the out of school lives of children is the *Centre psychopédagogique du Lycée Claude Bernard* at Paris. This Centre represents a developed concept of the Child Guidance Clinic as put forward in the United States and financed in Europe for a time by the Commonwealth Fund. It is situated within one of the large lycées and is under joint educational and psychiatric direction; and, through a considerable part-time and full-time staff of specialised educators, speech therapists, psychiatrists, social workers and psychologists, provides a very full range of diagnostic, therapeutic and remedial services. Although research is not one of its main functions, it has conducted some enquiries particularly into the emotional, intellectual and educational

1. Report from the Union Nationale des Associations régionales pour la Sauvegarde de l'Enfance et de l'Adolescence, M. Chabalar. The proportions for referrals cited in the text are very approximate since they are founded on an analysis of returns from seven Centres d'Observation and five Consultations, Dispensaires, etc. The figures for case loads of Consultations, Dispensaires and Centres Médico-pédagogiques are based on 25 returns.

problems of children at the stage of secondary education. It accepts cases referred by parents, by secondary schools, private doctors, school psychologists and the social services. Closely associated with it is the *"Ecole des Parents et des Maîtres"*, an organization which, in conjunction with the Faculty of Medecine of the University of the Sorbonne, undertakes parent education through a series of public lectures, a monthly journal, a series of pamphlets and through marriage guidance counselling, small parent discussion groups and individual consultations.

In the field of delinquency, the French Ministry of Justice through the *Direction de l'Education Surveillée* has instituted a psychological service which though still experimental is of considerable interest. Specially chosen and trained psychologists, either employed in one of the three residential Observation Centres established by the Ministry of Justice or in one of the two non-resident services attached respectively to the Children's Court of the Seine, and the Children's Court at Lyons, are charged with the full study of delinquents before their appearance in court, including a social case history, measurement of psycho-motor, intellectual and educational development, and an emotional and personality diagnosis. On the basis of this thorough examination, the psychologist makes a report to the judge both as to an explanation of the delinquency and as to future treatment. It is hoped that the service will be extended beyond the diagnostic function to include specialised reeducation and psychotherapy both in the institutions for delinquents and in the probation service. Perhaps the most interesting aspect of this scheme is that the psychologists employed by the Ministry of Justice are carefully selected for this work and in addition to their university theoretical and practical training, undergo a further practical course of six months to one year organized by the *Direction de l'Education Surveillée* itself.

In many ways the most interesting and well integrated of the French post war initiatives is the experiment of school psychologists. At the suggestion of the *Laboratoire de psychologie de l'enfant* of the *Institut de Psychologie* of the Sorbonne, University of Paris, and of the Director of the Educational services of the

Seine, sixteen posts as school psychologists in primary schools were established in 1946.[1] Two years later the Director of Secondary Education established 24 posts for the lycées in Paris. At the same time the experiment was extended to Grenoble and Lyons (for primary schools) and to Orléans (for secondary schools).

The important features of the experiment are that the school psychologist administratively and functionally belongs to the school or the group of schools in which he works. His task is to aid in the better adaptation of the pupil to the school and of the school to the pupil; and since this is regarded as a differentiation or specialisation of one of the functions of education, the school psychologist is the collaborator of the teacher and is indeed a teacher with specialist competence in the field of psychology applied to education. Much of this work consists in the continued study of the development of individual pupils, as well of the whole climate and atmosphere of the school. Nevertheless the improvement of educational method and the adaptation of the school to the pupil imply coordinated research. Hence, in the Paris region, and, to some extent, elsewhere, the university training centre assumes a responsibility for directing and coordinating the research work undertaken by the school psychologists and acts as a specialist service to which individual cases can be referred for a second opinion or more thorough examination.[2]

Some idea of the scope of the services given is indicated by the

1. The *Projet de la Réforme de l'Enseignement* published by the Ministry of Education in August 1947 contains the first official mention of the "*contrôle psychologique des élèves*". Before this however, a teacher trained at the Sorbonne went to Grenoble (1945) at the invitation of the then Inspecteur d'Académie de l'Isère, M. Richard. See "La psychologie scolaire en 1952", Zazzo, E. *Enfance* Nov.-Dec. 1952, no. 5. Special number.

2. The shortage of teachers in the primary schools and the fact that the service was started as an experiment with school psychologists seconded for the purpose from their official teaching posts without special status, has led (Sept. 13, 1954) to the recall of the fourteen psychologists working in the primary schools of the Seine to teaching posts. The experiment has been thus temporarily abandoned in the metropolitan region though continuing rather differently elsewhere.

figures published concerning the number and nature of the group and individual examinations undertaken in the schools. In the year 1952-53 for example the 14 psychologists working in primary schools examined over twelve thousand children of whom some 5,000 were seen individually. The bulk of these individual examinations (46.4 %) was undertaken to develop for each child a systematic psychological and educational record by which his progress through school could be followed and guided and a further quarter were concerned either with the specific educational guidance of individual children or with difficulties such as educational failure or retardation. The essential integration of the service with the schools is shown by the fact that 75 % of the requests for individual examinations came from teachers, head teachers and school inspectors.

The extension of such a service—which is based upon one psychologist to 1,000-1,500 pupils—clearly depends upon a recognition by education authorities of the needs which it fulfils and not less upon the availability of suitable candidates and suitable centres of training. Development is hindered in France as elsewhere by a lack of established and officially recognised standards of qualification and of a legally and administratively defined status for school psychologists. However certain universities, in the provinces as well as in Paris, have organized training not merely of a theoretical kind but also at a postgraduate professional level. The convention is beginning to grow up that the school psychologist, in addition to a basic university qualification in psychology, needs to have at least five years of successful teaching experience before entering upon a practical professional training in child development and applied educational psychology, at least part of which will take place in a functioning service. It is unlikely however that more than a few devoted pioneers will be attracted to a profession requiring so considerable a preparation unless, whilst retaining their status as members of the teaching profession, school psychologists are employed and paid as a special service.

ITALY[1]

In Italy, in spite of the early initiative of de Sanctis, and in spite of a considerable extension of health services, including the school medical service, little was undertaken before the outbreak of the last great war to develop services of psychology for the schools and children generally. There were individual initiatives, of course; but in general the educational authorities themselves were opposed, and indeed still remain cautious in their attitude. After the war, largely through the initiative of Carlo de Sanctis, Porta, Bollea, Busnelli and Bernini and through the visits of Bovet, Heuyer, Piaget, Rey and others to Italy, the question was reopened; and since 1946 there has been a considerable growth accompanied by the establishment of schools of social work, of faculties of psychology in the universities, and of psychiatric and pediatric clinics and hospitals. In the more strictly educational field, *Centri Didattici Nazionali* have been established to carry out studies and research work, in educational psychology, educational method and the like usually in connection with a particular branch or level of education; some of these have established demonstration services inside schools similar to those provided by the French school psychologists. Finally there are a number of national organizations for child and adult welfare, of local services depending upon provincial and communal authorities, and of university centres and clinics, which provide diagnostic, psychological services and in some cases undertake treatment.

Special educational provision is well developed in some aspects whilst much is still to be done in others. The first school for subnormal children in Italy was founded in 1898 but it was not until 1928[2] that official regulations were framed to set up

1. Based on the very full material assembled by the Italian National Commission for Unesco upon the basis of a nation-wide enquiry, including a report on special education drawn up by the Secretariat of the *Società Italiana per l'Assistenza Medico-psico-pedagogica ai minorati dell'Età Evolutiva*, and by Professor Giovanni Caló of the *Centro Didattico Nazionale di Studi e Documentazione*, Florence.

2. The Gentile reform—see article 230 of the *Testo Unico* and article 404 of the *Regolamento Generale* R.D. 26/4/1928 No. 1297.

special classes for backward children (*classi differenziati*)—of which there are now some 325 for 7,500 pupils and a waiting list of nearly 5,000—and training colleges—of which there are seven plus four other recognized courses—for teachers of the subnormal (*Scuole Magistrale Ortofrenice*). Five years later, with the passing of the administration of the school system from the local authorities to the state, special schools, day and boarding, were established. The special classes are attached to ordinary primary schools and take those children whose backwardness seems to be due mainly to environmental causes, and who therefore after two or three years may be expected to return to the ordinary school. The special schools are established for those children whose difficulties, intellectual, physiological, emotional or social, are more marked, and who therefore may be in need throughout their school lives of a specially adapted remedial education. Where it is possible to work with the family the school is a day boarding school[1] (*scuola autonoma*), of which there are twenty-two; for those children who have no family or have to be separated from their parents, there are some twenty boarding schools (*instituto medico-pedagogico*).

In addition there are eight other special institutions subventioned or maintained by the State. Most of these specialise, but some of them accept children with a wide range of difficulties in addition to, or other than, inferior intelligence—severely maladjusted, delinquent, epileptic, psychotic and the like. Other types of State special schools—for physically handicapped, blind, deaf, and delicate children—exist, mainly in the big towns. An idea of the balance of provision can be given by the figures for the city of Milan (population 1953: 2,559,201). Here, there is one large school (31 classes, 45 teachers, 371 pupils) for subnormal, markedly backward, pathologically maladjusted and delinquent children; there is a school for physically handicapped (19 classes, 29 teachers, 240 pupils); one school for tuberculous (5 classes, 5 teachers, 80 pupils); one for epileptic (12 classes, 16 teachers, 111 pupils): two schools for delicate children (45 classes, 57 teachers, 1,311 pupils in all);

1.   i.e. Children attend for the full day returning only to sleep at home.

a school (17 classes, 17 teachers, 200 pupils) for the blind and partially sighted, and another for the deaf and hard of hearing (28 classes, 34 teachers, 298 pupils). In addition to the provision made by the Ministry of Education, or receiving a State subvention, there are certain classes and schools maintained by private funds.

The teachers in the State schools, as well as a basic teaching qualification, possess a specialised diploma awarded after a one-year course in one of the *Scuole Magistrali Ortofrenice* or its recognised equivalent. These training colleges have been responsible, through their demonstration classes, for much research into teaching method and other problems, as have such institutions and organizations as the *Opera Nazionale Anormali Psichici Orfani di Guerra*, the *Instituti medico-pedagogi*, and particularly, the national association for medico-psycho-pedagogic assistance to the handicapped (*Società Italiana per l'Assistenza medico-psico-pedagogica ai Minorati dell'Età Evolutiva* (S.I.A.M.E.) which, as its name suggests, groups men and women from all the disciplines involved—medecine, psychology, education, social work, and law—and directs its attention to research, practical educational problems, and to the improvement of law and administration in the field.

It is against this background of the development of special education, of the immense problems left behind by the war, of the attempt since 1946 by various bodies to tackle some at least of the more urgent problems, and of the thorough enquiry into the structure and effectiveness of Italian education made by the Ministry of Education,[1] that the pattern of psychological services must be seen—tentative, experimental and expanding only cautiously in step with experiment, experience, and, in particular, with the availability of qualified staff.

Most of the work which is done ressembles the child guidance or psychiatric clinic in conception and is the offshot of services of child welfare or maternal and child health. For example the

1. *Le conclusioni dell'inchiesta nazionale per la riforma della scuola*, Ministero della Publica Istruzione, Roma, Commissione nazionale d'inchiesta per la Riforma della scuola, 1949.

Enti Nazionale per la Protezione Morale del Fanciullo has provincial commissions in every province which provide child and family welfare services, including a service of school social workers. Through the activity of these services, cases of difficult children are discovered and referred to the *Centri e Consultori Medico Psico Pedagogici* (CMPP) which exist in twenty-seven of the provinces. Most of these CMPP are situated in a school though some have independent buildings, and are staffed, typically, by a neuro-psychiatrist (part-time—three sessions weekly each of three hours), a psychologist and a social worker (full time). Their main task is diagnostic; in addition to special school placement, treatment is undertaken, for some ten per cent of cases (where staff and time permit). An idea of the case load is given by the fact that in 1953 twenty-two centres diagnosed rather more than three thousand new cases and saw nearly three thousand for the second or third time. Nearly half the children referred are sent by the school social service, and a further 12 or 13 per cent by the social services of the region. In certain districts, the CMPP undertake psychological examinations for the children's courts.

The *Opera Nazionale per la Maternità e l'Infanzia*, in addition to its maternal and child health services, has set up four psychological clinics in big towns and proposes to add seven more; certain others of its provincial branches have partial psychological services as part of their pediatric clinics.

Apart from these national bodies, some provincial administrations have Mental Health Dispensaries, some communal authorities (Milan, Reggio Emilia, Novara) have set up clinics and centres of child guidance, and two centres exist, one in the Institute of Psychology and one in the Pediatric Clinic of the University of Rome.

The services so far described are in the main under psychiatric direction and concerned principally with children who stand in need of direct psychological help. Though some of them undertake a small activity of educational guidance or collaborate with vocational guidance centres, few are staffed adequately to carry out the broader guidance tasks of a school psychological service or to undertake the fundamental research in child development and educational psychology which is necessary.

It is with this larger conception that the *Centro Didattico Nazionale per la Scuola Secondaria* is cautiously experimenting. Basing its concept generally upon a multidisciplinary approach, the centre has set up in some twenty-four secondary schools, differing types of service ranging from the complete team of psychiatrist, psychologist, social worker and specialised teacher to that of a school psychologist aided when necessary by the school medical officer and school social worker. Its aim is to try out which of the various types of organization most effectively meets the needs of the schools. In addition, for all the schools in Rome, it conducts a diagnostic and advisory service for children referred because of school failure. Under its direction a group of five psychologists has undertaken a coordinated research in Rome and Milan to make a detailed psychological and educational study of some 1,500 pupils in sixty classes. This is regarded as the first step in a programme of basic research necessary to develop an applied science of educational psychology as the background to the study of individual cases.

Of potentially equal importance is the Centre's contribution to the development of a concept of the tasks of the educational psychologist. In the course of the "*Giornate nazionale della Scuole Secondaria*" the Centre called together a group of psychologists to discuss this problem. The main suggestions made were: that the psychologist is excellently placed to aid the teacher in his task and to make the link with school medical and social services; he should undertake systematic research to determine the psychological bases of educational method; he should make the first diagnostic study of problem children referred to him by the school, and, where appropriate, carry out individual or group remedial work calling upon more specialised diagnostic or remedial services, if necessary; finally he should collaborate with the teacher in the task of educational and vocational guidance. These suggestions were complemented by an insistence upon the need for a better preparation of teachers themselves in child development and in applied social and educational psychology.

SPAIN[1]

In recent years, and particularly in Madrid and other large cities, the Spanish authorities have considerably developed their maternal and child health services. Within these, a very considerable effort has been made to raise the general level of parental care, especially of young children; and nurses and others have been trained to give advice and guidance to parents not only in matters of physical health but also in general child development.[2] As early as 1929 moreover services of vocational guidance were organized and have steadily developed. The National Institute of Psychotechnics in Madrid (*Instituto Nacional de Psicotecnia*), the Psychotechnic Institute of Barcelona, and vocational guidance offices in the principal provincial capitals provide between them, at least for the children in the towns, a service of guidance particularly in choice of work. They work mainly with technical and other vocational schools. In addition there are vocational guidance services maintained by local authorities (for example at Valencia) or by private organizations (e.g. the Altos Hornos of Bilbao). These services are staffed in each case usually by a teacher, a medical practitioner and a psychologist.

Certain children's courts (Barcelona, Madrid, Bilbao, Seville, etc.) have their own psychologists' office concerned with the examination of delinquents, and other cases which come before the tribunals. Finally we may mention the National School for Abnormal Children (*Escuela Nacional de anormales*) and other publicly and privately maintained schools for mentally and physically handicapped children.

Official opinion sees that these services are inadequate for the needs, particularly for those of parent education, the discovery and treatment of problem children and the development of vocational guidance in such a way as to link it with a sound system of educational guidance. The department of psychology

1. Based on information provided by the Spanish National Commission for Unesco.
2. See for example the service at Madrid (Director: Dr. Juan Bosch-Marin).

of the University of Madrid has begun to train educational psychologists, with the specific intention of developing the personnel necessary to a school psychological service. The Ministry of Education projects a law setting up a national organization of educational and vocational guidance based upon local, provincial and national centres, and with the task of making a psychological study of children as early as possible in their school life as the basis either of special education or subsequent educational and vocational guidance. Until however the University has trained sufficient psychological staff at an adequate level, it is not considered wise to attempt to set up so ambitious an organization.

SWEDEN[1]

Since the recent war, Sweden has initiated a comprehensive educational reform, the technical basis of which was a thorough psychological study of nearly the entire school population, mainly by means of group tests.[2] Apart from the questions of method and organization raised by this enquiry, by the school reform projects and by the recent educational acts, such matters as teacher training, special educational provision, educational and vocational guidance and the development of school psychological services have been the subject of study either by the Royal Board of Education or by various official committees. What follows therefore is an account of a transitional and developing situation.

Sweden is relatively well provided with special schools and classes for blind, deaf, physically handicapped, mentally subnormal and dull children. In addition, with considerable local variation, there exist classes for children with reading and writing

1. Based upon reports specially drawn up by Dr. Marta Björsjö, psychologist to the Royal Board of Education, Sweden and by the Swedish National Commission for Unesco.

2. See *School and Psychology*, Elmgren, J. Stockholm, Esselte, 1952. Düring, I., *The Swedish School Reform 1950*. Uppsala, Appelbergs Boktryckeriaktiebolag, 1951.

difficulties, for maladjusted children, for children who have reached school age but not school maturity, for the hard of hearing and for speech defectives. Classes for the partially sighted are contemplated. For teachers of almost all these groups, and especially for the blind, deaf and mentally subnormal, special training courses of one year or two years full time study exist, mainly organized by or under the direct supervision of the Board of Education. Almost all the teachers trained in these courses, or in the shorter ones organized for those who wish to teach the dull, or to take charge of remedial groups for those with special difficulty in reading and writing, have all the basic qualifications necessary to teach in primary schools and in most cases have a number of years teaching experience before they undertake further training.

In some districts preventive and advisory services are established. In certain places, for example, specially trained elementary school teachers administer school maturity tests which bear mainly on the intellectual development of school entrants and which allow the detection of children who may need help for a short period, placement in a special class or for whom school entry should be delayed.

Vocational guidance services in secondary schools are assured by vocational guidance officers from the Youth Employment Service (Royal Labour Board) in collaboration with teachers. The responsible authorities, in their instructions, stress the importance of close cooperation between teachers and vocational guidance officers—for example in discussing the pupil's school performance, his abilities, interests and prospects outside school. In the experimental comprehensive school (*enhetsskolan*) which will be found in some fifty of the 800 school districts, specially trained teachers are responsible for guidance during the last two years of the course and the children have the opportunity whilst still at school to gain experience of different jobs. Both nationally and locally, parent-teacher cooperation is organized with the participation of psychologists and psychiatrists, who, in addition are active in arranging lectures, courses, study groups and the like both for the benefit of parents and teachers and as part of the training of doctors, teachers, nurses and other similar key professions.

There is thus a considerable background activity and, in particular, the ordinary teacher in Sweden has a good general training in educational psychology and child development.

It is in this context that current provision for special services must be viewed. The bulk of these are of the Child Guidance type and exist in Stockholm, Gothenburg and in six of the twenty-four county districts. An idea of their size is given by the fact that between them they employ 30 psychiatrists and doctors, 21 psychologists and assistant psychologists, 29 social workers, 13 psychotherapists, and 15 specialised teachers. In addition there are three private child guidance clinics. School psychological services are less extensive, employing three psychiatrists and twelve psychologists only two of whom are full time, the rest having teaching duties. In addition to these specifically children's services financed either by the county councils, communes and larger cities, there are of course the psychiatric departments of the hospitals, and of the University Faculties of Medecine (Stockholm, Uppsala, Lund). Special mention should be made too of the Erica Medico-pedagogical Institute, which, as part of the practical training given to psychotherapists, maintains a guidance and treatment department for some 150-200 children yearly.

Some of the difficulties in the way of increasing and extending these services, and in particular of developing an effective school psychological service, are due to the fact that there is no organized training of psychologists in Sweden. Many of those at work are teachers who, to their basic qualifications, have added one or other of the specialised courses for teachers of handicapped children and in some cases have attended advanced university courses in psychology. A committee established by the Royal Board of Education[1] to study the whole problem of the establishment of services and the training of psychologists has just made its report. Among other things, it recommends

1. *Psykologisk Utbildning och Forskning*, Statens offentliga utredningar 1955: II. Ecklesiastikdepartementet. Stockholm 1955.

that a complete psychological training should take six years. Three of these are intended for fundamental university studies in psychology, pedagogy and sociology; then follows a year of practice and two further years mainly devoted to scientific methodical training under the guidance of working school psychologists or in a centre engaged in practical and research work. Teacher training and teaching experience are considered to be desirable preliminary qualifications.

Meanwhile the needs are known to exist: in 1952 for example it was estimated that to implement the regulation of 1945 establishing a psychological advisory centre in each county district, some 60-70 child psychiatrists would be needed; to develop and extend school psychological services with a minimum diagnostic and treatment task, it seems that some 70 chief psychologists and a considerable number of assistants are required. If the demands of the schools are to be met, this however is a minimum. An enquiry made by questionnaire to all schools and school authorities in the country in 1953 revealed that the problems of the differentiation of method and curricula, and of the adaptation of the school to the child are in the forefront of the teachers' preoccupations, and this demands research in educational psychology within which the more immediately pressing needs expressed by the teachers—for help with the difficult and failing children, for educational guidance at entry to school, at transfer to secondary school, and in choice of studies or of employment—take their appropriate place with some chance of a satisfactory solution.

SWITZERLAND[1]

Because of its federal organization and the independence of each of its twenty-two cantons, Switzerland presents a picture of great variety and unevenness. Yet with a total of 52 services

1. Based upon reports prepared by Dr. André Répond, Président du Comité national suisse d'hygiène mentale and by *Pro Infirmis*, for the Swiss National Commission, and by Professor Ernst Boesch, Professor of Psychology, University of the Saar.

of various kinds (1953) working in the main city centres but extending their activities into the smaller towns and the country-side, it is one of the countries in Europe having the fullest development. It was also, as will be recalled from earlier remarks, one of the pioneers of psychological services, with the initiatives of Claparède in Geneva in 1912 and of Hegg in Berne in 1920. Nevertheless it is calculated that for example in the Valais (population 160,000) which is one of the best provided cantons having already a service staffed by one full-time and two part-time psychiatrists, three to four non-medical psycho-therapeutic staff and a social worker, a further fifteen psycho-logists and psychotherapists would be necessary to operate a full service for school children. For Zurich some thirty psychological staff would be necessary by the same criteria.

A similar picture presents itself in the field of special education. Throughout the country, residential schools and institutions exist for physically and mentally handicapped children, for the maladjusted, and for speech defectives. There is also a consider-able activity of remedial education (*heilpädagogik*) not only for the dull and subnormal but for the retarded and educationally backward. Nevertheless it is calculated that provision should be made for some 4-6 % of the population of school age, i.e. for about 18-28,000 children—whereas, currently, provision is made for 6,274 children, or for only about one third of those held to need special education.

Certain towns, for example Bâle (6.04 %) and Geneva (3.95 %) are, of course, well above the national average and within measurable distance of having a fully sufficient provision. All these special institutions are grouped in the Swiss Association "Pro Infirmis" though many of them depend upon the *Société suisse d'utilité publique* or upon cantonal, educational or health authorities.

To complete this background it may be remarked that the basic training of many Swiss primary and secondary school teachers contains a considerable element of child study and educational psychology and that many of the University centres notably Geneva, Zurich and Bâle, have advanced courses for experienced teachers who wish to specialise in educational psychology, for those who wish to teach the subnormal, and for those who wish to become educational psychologists. As a research centre in child study, first under the leadership of Claparède, and subsequently under that of Piaget, the Institut des Sciences de l'Education of the University of Geneva is too well known to need mention.

The psychological services of the country are of three main types: those which form part of adult psychiatric services (*consultations de psychiatrie infantile*); services inspired by the Child Guidance formula (*services médico-pédagogiques*); and school psychological services of various complete or partial forms (*Consultations de pédagogie curative, Services d'observation des écoles, Services psychologiques scolaires*, etc.).

Of the first we may cite as an example the *Consultation de psychiatrie infantile* of the *polyclinique universitaire de Zurich*. This service which also serves university training purposes, is staffed by a director, two to three psychiatrists, a psychologist and a social worker. One of its medical staff is at the same time director of an observation home in Zurich for maladjusted children. The service is essentially occupied with children having severe problems of behaviour or development, and does not normally work with the schools. The town of Zurich however possesses a school psychological service integrated with the school medical service and a *Consultation de pédagogie curative* (*Heilpadägogik*) attached also to the University.

Of the services which base themselves upon the child guidance clinic formula, that is upon a team of psychologist, psychiatrist and social worker, the most highly developed is that founded in 1930 by Dr. André Répond in the Canton du Valais. Based on psychoanalytic principles including a considerable activity of psychotherapy with children, the service operates from the Maison de Santé de Malevoz and has travelling consultations in most of the canton, reaching even the more remote villages. Its objectives are mainly the discovery and treatment of abnormal children, the prevention of maladjustment and the arousing of interest in such problems. Where necessary, it works with schools but it does not, except incidentally, undertake direct preventive or constructive work through the educational guidance of normal children or through the application of mental health principles to common problems of the classroom or of educational methods. Similar services exist elsewhere in Switzerland, particularly in the French and Italian speaking areas, e.g. the cantons of Vaud, Neuchatel, Tessin.

The school psychological services are very varied in their structure and more or less complete in the services which they are able to offer. The *Consultation pédagogique de la ville de Berne*, for example, directed by Dr. Hegg, the educational psychologist who founded it in 1920, is an autonomous part of the school medical service: its principal tasks are those of psychological adviser to the schools, the discovery, examination, and treatment—by psychotherapy, remedial education and other means—of difficult or retarded children and the general psychological supervision of the special classes of the town. Its action is limited by the smallness of its staff (one psychologist as director, one assistant psychologist and a social worker), but nevertheless includes a good deal of in-training of teachers, general educational and vocational guidance and parent education. In the canton of Berne, in each educational district, a specialized teacher with a university training undertakes a service of educational psychology for the schools. A rather similar formula is that of Lucerne where the Professor of Education at the training college (Dr. Simmen) has gathered together and trained a group of 18 primary school teachers to undertake the discovery and examination of problem children and to provide a service of educational guidance in the schools.

The education authorities of the city of Geneva, inspired in part by the work of the Institut des Sciences d'éducation, set up in 1930 a "*Service d'observation des écoles*" which in many ways seems to meet most of the needs of the schools. It is directed by a psychologist who is at the same time inspector of special schools and classes. He is assisted by a part-time (10 hours a week) psychiatrist, a full-time assistant psychologist, a social worker and a speech therapist. The service provides educational and vocational guidance, arranges for remedial education or other forms of treatment, the discovery and examination of problem children, especially at the nursery school stage and acts as psychological and educational adviser to the special schools and classes. As well as with the schools, it works closely with the child welfare services of the city and with the children's courts.

Finally we may mention a form of organization which has proved successful in districts of scattered population—the travelling school psychological service. With similar objectives to the services described above, the school psychological service of St. Gall, for example, works mainly in the schools of the canton and serves a school population of some 50,000 children. Originally (1939) staffed with one psychologist only, it now has two full-time psychologists and a social worker. Essentially it is an advisory service to the teachers and to the education authorities, with whom the decision as to the action to be taken rests; and its activity though widespread, is limited especially, on the remedial side, by the smallness of its staff.

Almost all the types of services described undertake functions of a wider kind than that of examining and treating children with difficulties of one kind or another. Most of them carry on a considerable activity of public education in the principles of mental hygiene; many run short training courses for teachers; some, for example, the *Service médico-pédagogique Valaisan*, provide a full practical training for child psychiatrists, psychologists, psychotherapists and social workers; others, apart from parent guidance in connection with specific children, undertake the general education of parents; and most collaborate as occasion demands with other services concerned with the welfare of children. Since the end of the last war, there has been a steady increase in services and a widening of their scope to include more preventive and constructive activity both through the schools and in the training of teachers. The French concept of an *Ecole des Parents* has found an echo in Geneva and Lausanne where, in addition to lectures and discussion groups, parents can obtain consultative services; and in one or two other centres—for example Winterthur—attempts have been made to associate the psychological education of young mothers with physical health services.

The existing services however remain, according to informed opinion, insufficient in extent and—quite rightly—experimental in their development, depending largely for their direction and preoccupations upon local needs and conceptions and upon the skill and insight of their staff.

THE UNITED KINGDOM[1]

From the outset, British educational psychology emphasised social factors, no doubt because the Industrial Revolution had left behind it great social problems and because public spirited people like Charles Booth, the Webbs and others realized the significance of social handicaps and their effects upon school children. McDougall among others was greatly influenced by this movement, and his most widely read work was entitled "*Social Psychology*".[2] As a consequence of this and of the general English educational tradition, a peculiarity of psychological work in England from the start has been the emphasis on remedial training rather than on treatment—an approach via the science of educational and social psychology rather than via medical psychology. Even those psychologists favourable to psycho-analytic concepts placed more emphasis upon re-education than was usual elsewhere.

Since the turn of the century the education departments of the Universities, as well as undertaking the training and further training, particularly, of secondary school teachers, have increasingly interested themselves in educational research, educational psychology and the science of child development.

1. Based by the editor on information supplied by the British Psychological Society, "Memorandum on the Schools Psychological Services in Europe"; the National Association for Mental Health "Psychological Services for Children, particularly in Schools. The existing Psychological Services for Children"; and on the various printed sources acknowledged in the text. What follows refers more particularly to England and Wales.

2. First published in 1906.

Much indeed of the research, basic to practical services of child guidance and educational guidance, has been the work of professors of education and their postgraduate students.[1] Similarly, following the example of the early pioneers,[2] certain University Departments of Education and of Psychology between the two wars, set up demonstration educational and and psychological services and clinics as part of their practical training programmes.[3] After the second world war, many English Universities brought about an even closer association between practising teachers, local education authorities, teacher training colleges and the Universities. In some cases, through the creation of Institutes of Education in which all those concerned with education in a considerable area participate, this has led to a considerable expansion of research facilities to the development of post-graduate training courses[4] for specialised teachers and for educational psychologists, and to the establishment of further experimental psychological services of different types.[5]

It is thus fair to say that a minimum knowledge of child development and of the psychology of education is well spread among teachers in the United Kingdom; in addition, a considerable proportion of teachers and educational administrators, through short courses run by University extra-mural departments and through the opportunities offered for part-time and full-time study for higher degrees in Education, have received a theoretical and practical training in applied psychology and research.[6] The British Psychological Society, founded early in

1. See for example the *List of researches in Education and Psychology* and *A Second List of researches in Education and Educational Psychology*, Blackwell, A. M., London, Newnes Educational Publishing Co., 1952.

2. See p. 15.

3. e.g. University College London, Department of Psychology, (Professor Burt), Glasgow University (Dr. Boyd & Professor Drever), Aberdeen University (Professor R. Knight and Dr. N. Walker).

4. e.g. the courses at Manchester, London, Birmingham and Leeds in applied educational psychology for practising teachers.

5. e.g. the Remedial Education Centre at Birminghan, the Children's Centre at Leeds.

6. For a critical discussion see Vernon P.E. "Postgraduate training of

the century, now has a membership of more than two thousand among whom the largest group is directly or indirectly concerned with education, and outside the Society there are many teachers, administrators and training college staff whose knowledge of psychology is considerable though not complete.

The *British Journal of Educational Psychology*, jointly sponsored by the British Psychological Society and by the Association of Teachers in Colleges and Departments of Education has a circulation of over two thousand copies inside the United Kingdom.[1] In addition there are two national research institutions concerned with enquiries into the psychological aspects of education—the Scottish Council for Research in Education[2] and the National Foundation for Educational Research in England and Wales[3]—each of which involves practising teachers in ongoing research work and publishes the results either in the form of monographs or through the professional journals.

Parallel with this interest in psychology applied to practical problems of education, there has been a marked trend, since before the first world war, towards an increasing differentiation of educational provision. This has been expressed on the one hand in the development of different kinds of secondary education in England especially since the English Education Act of 1944, and in a diversified system of special schools and classes for children with physical, mental, or social handicaps, such that their needs cannot adequately be met in the ordinary school.

This diversification of provision has, not unexpectedly, accentuated the need for adequate guidance of normal children and adolescents, between schools, classes or courses, and

Teachers in Psychology", *Brit. Journ. of Ed. Psych., Vol. XX, Part.* 3, Nov. 1950.

1. See also: Vernon P. E. *Modern Educational Psychology as a Science*, University of London Institute of Education, 1950.

2. For an account of its work, see: *The Scottish Council for Research in Education*; *Its Aims and Activities*. University of London Press, London, 1953.

3. See the biannual *Bulletins* of The National Foundation for Educational Research in England and Wales, published by the Foundation.

within the schools themselves. As one of the means of aiding teachers and others in this task, cumulative school record cards containing details of the educational progress, interests, character and personality traits of each child have been developed.[1] Their use is by no means universal[2]; the cards themselves are not of a standard pattern; and their value is directly dependent upon the knowledge, insight and skill of the teachers using them. Nevertheless, some Local Education Authorities have made them obligatory at least in their primary schools and, through a vigorous programme of research on the one hand and of the in-training of their teachers on the other, have developed them as an integral part of a system of effective guidance.

The crucial general problem of guidance in the English educational system however has always been that of the choice of secondary studies, particularly of those able to profit from an academic education. This problem became acute with the Education Act of 1944 which made all education after the age of eleven free in the state maintained schools. Owing to the greater prestige of the Secondary "Grammar" Schools which cater for the abler pupils and prepare for entry to the Universities and to the professions and to a shortage of accommodation in them as compared with the modern and technical schools, this allocation at eleven took on, and still bears, more the appearance of selection than of guidance. Much effort has been devoted to developing a system which shall be valid in prognosticating success; which shall be fair in that a child shall get a chance of academic education if he is suitable for it, irrespective of his social or educational history; and which shall be acceptable to parents. The system adopted by most local education authorities in England is to apply to all children between the

1. See for example: Hamley, R. et al., *The Educational Guidance of the School Child;* Fleming, C. M., *Cumulative Records: Notes on their Content and Uses*, London, U.L.P.

2. It will be remembered that the main responsibility for the administration of Education in the United Kingdom lies with the Local Education Authorities of the towns and counties. They enjoy a considerable degree of autonomy which permits local experiment and initiative.

ages of ten and eleven a series of standardized tests of educable capacity, of English and of Arithmetic, on the results of which they are allotted to the Grammar, Secondary Technical or Secondary Modern schools according to the numbers of places available. The examination is thus competitive—in some places heavily so—and while many of the major and minor sources of error have been eliminated by improvements in the technique of examining, few educationists are fully satisfied that the present system is more than making the best of a difficult job. Many education authorities are experimenting with variations on this basic method, including the use of individual psychological examinations for children on the borderlines, interviews, and the use of cumulative school record cards as an additional criterion or even as a substitute for the examination.[1] [2]

As elsewhere in Europe, the earliest provision for handicapped children goes back to the turn of the century or before and was made by independent benevolent bodies for the blind, the deaf, the grossly physically handicapped and the markedly mentally subnormal. Between the two wars and especially since 1945, there has been a marked expansion within the state system both

1.   "Eleven plus selection" as it is called has been the subject of an immense amount of research of which a full bibliography would fill many pages. The reader is referred to the following representative titles: "Symposium on the Selection of Pupils for Different Types of Secondary School", *Brit. Journ. Ed. Psych.* 1947–50; W. McClelland, *Selection for Secondary Education*, Scottish Council for Research in Education, London, Univ. of London Press, 1942; National Union of Teachers, *Transfer from Primary to Secondary School*, London, Evans Bros., 1949; A. F. Watts and P. Slater, *The Allocation of Primary School Leavers to Courses of Secondary Education*, London, Nat. Found. For Ed. Research, 1950.
    The British Psychological Society is at present preparing a memorandum on this subject, and the above must not be taken to represent its views.
2.   In Scotland there are certain differences. For example. Education Authorities, so long as sufficient provision for free educational facilities is made in their area, may maintain some fee paying primary and secondary schools. There are proportionately rather more facilities for academic secondary education in Scotland than in England and many more of the Scottish Secondary schools are comprehensive schools providing three and five or six year courses differentiated according to the needs and capacities of the pupils. More over the age of transfer tends to be later: $11\frac{1}{2}$–$12\frac{1}{2}$

of the number of places available as well as a formal recognition of new categories. The English Education Act of 1944[1] confers on parents the right to ask for the examination of any of their children aged two or more to see if they require special educational treatment. The Education Authority is bound to have this examination carried out and if the child requires special educational treatment, even before compulsory school age, this must be provided if the parent so wishes. However most children who need special treatment are discovered after they have begun school (5 years) and then usually through the observations of their teachers. The school medical and psychological services carry out the necessary examinations, and advise the Local Education Authority which has the power to enforce attendance at a special school or class if necessary.

This statutory duty to discover all children needing special help, and the increasing emphasis upon the need for careful examination and guidance which began well before the second world war, led to the recognition of several broad classes of children in need of an adapted education and to the growth of a considerable number of different kinds of school, some of them directly maintained by Local Education Authorities, some of them financed by voluntary bodies with direct or indirect state assistance. In 1945, the English Ministry of Education recognized ten broad classifications of handicapped children; the blind, the partially sighted, the deaf, the partially deaf, the delicate, the educationnally subnormal, the epileptic, the maladjusted, the physically handicapped and those with speech defects. It was not intended that all the children falling into any one of these categories should attend a special school; nor that the schools or classes developed should rigidly correspond to any particular category. This may be illustrated by the category of the "educationally subnormal". It is estimated that some ten per cent of children fall into this category, the criterion for inclusion in which is that the child, for whatever reason, is retarded *educationally*. This retardation may be due to intellec-

1. See Ministry of Education Pamphlet No. 5. *Special Educational Treatment*, London H.M.S.O. 1956.

tual subnormality, irregular school attendance, specific difficulties in reading or in arithmetic, social or personal maladjustment or to other causes. Whether the child attends a special
school for children of subnormal intelligence, whether he
attends a special class in an ordinary school, or whether he
receives some form of individual help, will depend upon local
facilities and upon a careful study of his case during the process
of his education.

The category of "maladjusted children" is also a wide and
inclusive one covering many kinds and types of emotional,
personal, or social difficulties. For such children, day and
boarding schools are provided, some specialised in a particular
kind of maladjustment; there are, too, hostels from which the
children go to ordinary schools, special remedial groups in
child guidance centres or in ordinary schools, and so on. In
the education of physically handicapped there have been several
recent developments, notably the provision of specially conceived schools for cerebrally palsied children; day and boarding
schools for children with multiple handicaps and schools which
cater for different specific types of physical and mental handicaps.

The expansion of these special educational services has been
hindered by the evident financial cost of provision and by the
lack of suitably trained teachers. No one would say that all
needs are satisfied and, while the large towns are fairly well
served, there are parts of the country which are not reached.
Training facilities for specialised teachers are inadequate. The
blind are relatively well served by the courses conducted by the
College of Teachers of the Blind, and the Department for the
Education of the Deaf at the University of Manchester has been
training specialist teachers of the deaf since well before the last
war. One year courses for teachers of the educationally subnormal now exist in certain University teacher training departments;
and the courses in Child Development and Remedial Education
conducted by some of the Institutes of Education for experienced
teachers provide a sound basis of professional knowledge and
skill for those who wish to teach maladjusted children. The
Ministry of Education itself and many local education authori-

ties conduct short courses for teachers to increase the level of knowledge and understanding in the general field of special educational provision. It is likely too that in the near future as the result of a ministerial advisory committee[1] there may be an improvement in the supply and training of teachers for handicapped pupils in England.

An idea of the extent of the special educational provision currently made is given by the fact that in Scotland in 1953[2] for a population of some 830,000 children of school age some 10,000 children were being educated in special schools and classes. This does not include those for whom special arrangements are made in ordinary schools without these constituting a special class; nor does it include the population of schools for delinquent children. In England and Wales, with a school population somewhat above six million, provision is made in 680 special schools alone (maintained and voluntary) for rather more than 54,000 children.[3] Official estimates of the proportions of children needing some form of special educational treatment —not necessarily in special schools or classes—vary between about 10 per cent to as much as 15-16 per cent of the school population. From these estimates the numbers of the delinquent are omitted.[4] It will be seen that, even allowing for the fact that,

1.   Ministry of Education. *National Advisory Council on the Training and Supply of Teachers of Handicapped Pupils: Fourth Report*, London H.M.S.O., 1954.

2.   Secretary of State for Scotland: *Education in Scotland in* 1953. Edinburgh, H.M.S.O., 1954.

3.   Ministry of Education (U.K.) *Education in* 1953. London, H.M.S.O., 1954.

4.   Delinquent children and adolescents may be sent to Approved Schools. These are under the authority of the Home Office and not that of the Ministry of Education. A recent development has been the setting up of Classifying Centres where delinquent children are kept for a period under psychological observation before being allocated to the Approved School which seems most suitable to their particular case. Some psychological observation is also carried out—frequently by the staff of the Child Guidance clinic or centre—in Remand Homes where children who cannot be left in their homes or who have been arrested may be sent before they appear in the Children's Courts.

for example, many of the largest group of all, the educationally subnormal, will be accomodated in ordinary schools with a specially adapted curriculum, there is still a considerable gap between what is considered desirable and what has so far been possible.

In England it is estimated that some 20,500 children are awaiting places in special schools.

It is into the pattern rather summarily described above, and with local and national differences, that the various services of child guidance fit. Here it should be remarked that, although there are somewhere between two and three hundred child guidance clinics, child guidance centres, services of remedial education, child psychiatric clinics and the like in England[1] and rather more than thirty in Scotland, such services are in many cases incomplete in one or other respect. Moreover many of the tasks of educational guidance for ordinary children, research into child development and its applications to the improvement of education, parent education, constructive and preventive mental health work in the schools are either not carried out at all or are frequently undertaken independently of the official services. In part this is because the basic concepts and emphasis of these services are not yet fully worked out; in part because, administratively, similar services may depend either upon the health or upon the education services; and in part it is because of a considerable cleavage of opinion between those who see psychological services as having a primarily psychiatric direction with emphasis upon the treatment of the abnormal and those who conceive of them as a broader service of psychological help to the school system with an emphasis upon remedial education rather than principally upon the examination and treatment of maladjusted children.

Administratively there are a number of more or less satisfactory compromises. Child psychiatric clinics, out-patient depart-

1. National Association for Mental Health. *Child Guidance Clinics in England and Wales*, 1955. London, N.A.M.H. ,1955. This is an incomplete list and concentrates principally upon those which are more or less based upon the classical child guidance formula.

ments of mental hospitals or general hospitals which undertake psychological work with children, and Child Guidance clinics wholly or partly maintained by the Health Service tend to have a full or part-time medical director. This director may or may not be a qualified child psychiatrist, and he is frequently assisted by psychiatric consultants and physicians. Almost invariably there is one or more full-time psychiatric social workers, many of whom, as well as working with parents, undertake play-therapy. In addition, those clinics, which give a direct service to the education authorities or do much work with children of school age, usually employ one or more full-time educational psychologists who, apart from the psychological and educational examination of children which is part of the normal routine, may undertake remedial education, play therapy, act as consultants to special schools, and generally maintain the contacts with the schools and the education authorities. Not infrequently where the psychiatrically oriented clinic has no full-time psychologist, it is the educational psychologist employed by the local education authority who undertakes the necessary work.

Child Guidance clinics and Child psychiatric clinics partly or wholly maintained by the Local Education authorities are frequently under the nominal or actual direction of the school medical officer, or of a full-time or, more usually, a part-time psychiatrist employed by the Health Service. In these cases effective direction is usually in the hands of the senior educational psychologist, and the staff is completed by one or more social workers, sometimes by non-medical psycho-therapists and by specially trained remedial teachers. Such clinics, because they are administratively more closely linked with the educational system and because the psychologist is in effective charge, have much closer, more frequent and more fruitful contacts with the schools than would be expected of hospital or other clinics outside the educational service.

Some education authorities in England and Wales and many in Scotland[1] where Child Guidance has been from its inception

1.   See McCallum, C. M. "Child Guidance in Scotland" *British Journal Ed. Psych. Vol. XXII, Part* 2., 1952.

an educational service, believe that what before all else is necessary is a service of a preventive, advisory and remedial kind for the schools. They have therefore tended to establish, under the direction of an educational psychologist, a school psychological service or a Child Guidance Centre the main preoccupation of which is not with serious maladjustment but with the far greater numbers of children who experience difficulties of personal, social and educational adjustment.[1] This point of view has been strongly endorsed by the Association of Education Committees' Sub-committee on Child Guidance[2] and as strongly attacked by various psychiatric professional bodies.

These school psychological services, Child Guidance centres, or Educational centres, as they are variously called, are usually wholly maintained by the local education authority. Their full-time staff consists, according to their size, of one or more educational psychologists, one or more social workers, remedial teachers, speech reeducators and the like. Among their tasks is that of the ascertainment of children in need of special educational treatment, including the educationally subnormal and the emotionally maladjusted, consultative work with the special schools and classes set up by the education authorities, general educational, and sometimes, vocational guidance, work with parents individually or through parent-teacher associations, and advisory work with teachers in the ordinary schools. Such services or centres invariably have access to the school medical service and can obtain any necessary psychiatric help either on a consultant basis or through psychiatric clinics attached to the Health Service. Sometimes they contain or are closely associated with a system of remedial teachers or remedial classes.

Next perhaps to the expansion of all kinds of services for

1.   "In 1939, 17 clinics were wholly and 5 partly maintained by local education authorities. Ten years later, in 1949, 73 local education authorities maintained one or more Child Guidance Centres". Roneotyped report of the National Ass. for Mental Health, 1952.

2.   See Alexander, W. P. "Notes on Child Guidance. Report of the Child Guidance Subcommittee", *Education*, 15 Feb. 1946, and *The Child Guidance Service in Principle and in Fact*, Sheffield, 1943

maladjusted children, the development of remedial education has been the most striking feature since the war. Among the groups of children needing special educational treatment, the educationally subnormal were recognized officially[1] to be the most numerous. Furthermore many local education authorities became alarmed at the results of age group surveys by means of standardized tests of attainment and ability which indicated a considerable proportion of educational backwardness even among children of normal or superior innate ability, and a number of children who though not technically backward, were in fact retarded as compared with their capacity. Some of this was due to the disturbance of education during 1939-45, but it was, and still is, felt that here is a problem which though reduced by a return to more normal conditions, is likely to remain.[2] Much research into the general problems had been undertaken between the wars on the basis of which the University of Birmingham Institute of Education, immediately after the end of the war, began a study of educational retardation which developed into its Remedial Education Centre opened officially in 1948.[3] This centre provided the practical basis for a one year course for experienced teachers in child development with, however, special reference to remedial education for bright children experiencing educational difficulties. Experienced teachers trained by the University Institute in 1946, 1947 and later, found employment with local education authorities as specialist advisers some of them setting up remedial education centres or services. In 1952 a survey of 116 local education authorities revealed that 32 of them had special identification procedures (usually by means of school record cards, or periodic age-group testing), 53 gave assistance by means of educational guidance services, in the form of specialists who visit the schools, 23 provided remedial teaching in schools or child guidance

1.   *Special Educational Treatment*. Ministry of Education (U.K.) Pamphlet No. 5, H.M.S.O 1946.
2.   See Ministry of Education, U.K., *Reading Ability*, H.M.S.O., 1950.
3.   See Schonell F. J., & Wall W. D., "The Remedial Education Centre" *Educational Review Vol. II Pt.* 1. 1949.

centres, 7 provided special remedial centres, and 29 made provision for bright retarded children in their classes for the backward.[1] The survey also revealed that the expansion of the service was greatly hindered by the lack of suitably-trained staff.

In addition to the above services, many local education authorities, especially the larger ones, employ a chief educational psychologist in a mainly coordinating and advisory role. As well as some work in a Child Guidance Clinic or Centre, supervision of remedial education, consultant work in the special schools or classes, advice on the use of mental tests for school survey purposes or for eleven plus selection, he has the general task of advising the chief education officer on all psychological matters relating to the schools, arranging for or taking part in the short in-service training courses for teachers which many authorities arrange and a considerable variety of other work.

It is coming to be agreed in England that while the classic conception of the child guidance clinic with its threefold team of psychologist, psychiatrist and social worker should be preserved, it is not sufficient alone to meet all the problems of the schools in the most economical manner. This team is peculiarly adapted to the diagnosis and treatment of severe maladjustment and psychosis in children; but, while there are theoretical and professional disagreements as to what constitutes maladjustment demanding psychiatric diagnosis and treatment, there is at least tacit accord that many school problems—and those from the teachers' point of view the most urgent—fall into the province of remedial education and educational psychology. Hence while Child Guidance Clinics and especially Child Guidance Centres have increased markedly in numbers since 1930, progressive education authorities have tended more and more to supplement their work with a variety of special psychological and educational staff. Sometimes these staff are formally integrated with the Child Guidance Clinic or Centre into a thoroughly comprehensive service; sometimes they exist side

1. See Collins, J. E., "Remedial Educational Provision for Children of Average and Above Average Intelligence" *Educational Review*, *Vol. 6*, *Nos. 1, 2 and* 3, 1954.

by side with more or less of cooperation according to personalities and local circumstances. The Committee of Professional
Psychologists (Mental Health) of the British Psychological
Society advocated that a complete psychological service for
schools should include a Child Guidance Centre, and should
provide advisory services to Children's Departments[1], to parents,
to Welfare Clinics, as well as to ordinary and special schools;
it should also be responsible for services of educational and
vocational guidance and of remedial education, as well as
having close contact with hostels and schools for maladjusted
children and a Child Psychiatric or Child Guidance Clinic.
It considered that a chief educational psychologist should be
responsible for the preventive and guidance services and that
in the special educational field, including the treatment of
maladjusted children, he should collaborate with the school
health service and through that have access to outside specialist
medical services as these may be necessary. This is the pattern
which predominates in Scotland, and is exceptionally well
embodied in the services provided by the Corporation of
Glasgow, Education Department, and the City of Aberdeen.[2]
Similar organizations are to be found in Barrow-in-Furness,
Birmingham, Coventry, Leeds, Leicester, Middlesborough,
Sheffield, the West Riding of Yorkshire and elsewhere in
England. A special Committee set up by the Ministry of Education to consider the future development of services for maladjusted children has cautiously recommended an extension of this
formula as did the Advisory Council on Education in Scotland.[3]

1.   There is a special service of Children's Officers, set up under the
Home Office, to deal with all children who either have no parent or guardian,
or who have been committed by the Courts to the care of the local authority.
Some of these children's officers are psychologists by training, others are
social workers, others have been trained in Child Care Courses conducted
by Universities or by the Home Office.

2.   See McCallum, C. M. "Child Guidance in Scotland", *Brit. Journ.
Ed. Psych. Vol. XXII*, Part 2., 1952.

3.   Ministry of Education (U.K) *Report of the Committee on Maladjusted
Children* London, H.M.S.O. 1955 esp. Chapter VI. *Report on Pupils who
are maladjusted because of social handicaps*, Advisory Council on Education
in Scotland, H.M.S.O., Cmd. 8428.

Little has so far been said of vocational guidance, apart from the work which is incidental to some psychological services, child guidance centres or clinics. Administratively every local education authority has the right to develop a juvenile employment service; if it does not choose to exercise this right, the task is undertaken by the local organization of the Ministry of Labour.[1] Each area in England has a Juvenile Advisory Committee concerned with youth matters and a Juvenile Employment Committee representing the authorities, the schools and the employers, the trade unions and welfare organizations. This latter committee helps and advises the Youth Employment Officers who are available in most areas for the guidance of school leavers. A very considerable range of pamphlets has been prepared giving details of careers in industry, commerce and the professions with particulars of the educational levels, and personal qualities required, the kind of training available and so on. Not infrequently the youth employment officers visit the schools, speak to the school leavers and their parents and hold with the staff, parents, and children a "choice of employment conference". Little general attempt is made at a systematic use of standardized tests for vocational guidance, although a number of experimental schemes have been set up and have given striking results.[2] The National Institute of Industrial Psychology[3] (N.I.I.P.) which has pioneered scientific vocational guidance in England since its vocational guidance department was organized by Burt in 1923, has done much to prepare for the considerable postwar development and to foster the growth

1. About 80% of L.E.As. in England, since the Employment and Training Act of 1948, have their own youth employment service to which *all* school leavers are compulsorily notified.

2. See for example: (a) *A Study in Vocational Guidance*, I.F.R.B., London, H.M.S.O., 1926; (b) Allen & Smith: *The Value of Vocational Tests as Aids in the Choice of Employment*, First Report, 1932, Second Report, 1940. *Scientific Vocational Guidance and its value to the Choice of Employment Work of a Local Education Authority*, 1944. Birmingham, City of Birmingham Education Authority; (c) The publications in the N.I.I.P., Journal *Occupational Psychology* (especially April/May, 1935 and following).

3. See: Lock, H. F. "The National Institute of Industrial Psychology" *Yearbook of Education* 1955. London, Evans Bros, 1955.

of official as well as voluntary services. In the secondary grammar schools and in the public schools, Careers Masters or
Mistresses[1]—many of them trained in short courses conducted
by the N.I.I.P.—make themselves responsible for continuous
guidance and information towards the end of the school career
and for cooperation with the Youth Employment Service on
the basis of a carefully compiled and cumulative school record
card.

In the country there are, in addition to the general services
described above, a number of unique institutions, publicly
maintained or privately endowed, which have either a special
scientific point of view or a particular function. Mention has
already been made of the *Remedial Education Centre* at the
University of Birmingham Institute of Education and of the
National Institute of Industrial Psychology. The *Institute for the
Scientific Study and Treatment of Delinquency* should also be
recorded. As its name implies, it is concerned with the prevention
of delinquency through child and parent guidance and with
the treatment and care of delinquents.

Even more widely known in Europe is the *Tavistock Clinic*
which as well as undertaking the diagnosis and treatment of
severe maladjustment in children and adolescents through its
"Department for Children and Parents", has a considerable
training and research function. The *Maudsley Hospital* as well
as having a Children's Department has a psychological and
psychiatric research centre forming part of the Institute of
Psychiatry, University of London, and provides training for
clinical psychologists and child psychiatrists leading to the
award of a University Diploma. Similar research centres exist
elsewhere notably at the Crichton Royal Hospital, Dumfries,
Scotland. The Hampstead Child Therapy Clinic, a private
organization, directed by Anna Freud, is one of the two centres
for the training of play therapists (the other is the Tavistock
Clinic).

We may in conclusion briefly indicate the nature of the

1. See: King, H. R., "Vocational Guidance for School Pupils", United
Kingdom, ibid.

training of educational psychologists in the United Kingdom. The Committee of Professional Psychologists (Mental Health), an organ of the British Psychological Society, has a membership of rather more than three hundred and fifty psychologists. It has laid down certain minimum standards of qualification for those educational psychologists to whom it grants recognition and membership. These are (a) In England[1]: a University education in Psychology to the level of a good first degree or its equivalent, training as a teacher, and two years experience either of teaching or some other work with normal children, and a special practical professional training of one year in clinical and educational diagnostic and remedial work.[2] Recognition is not normally granted until the candidate has worked, after qualification, for at least one year as assistant to a fully qualified educational psychologist. (b) In Scotland—the post-graduate University degree of B. Ed. in educational psychology constitutes the basis of recognition by the educational authorities and much of the practical training is given on the job by functioning services. The Committee of Professional Psychologists grants recognition only to candidates who in addition to this basic training and experience have satisfactorily completed two years practical work under the supervision of a principal psychologist.

Training facilities, in England at all events, are insufficient and only 20-30 educational psychologists are trained each year. The training with the longest history is that given by the Department of Psychology. University College, London, which is recognized by a University Diploma. The National Association for Mental Health (which incorporates the Child Guidance Training Council) gives grants to students for training either at the Child Guidance Training Centre, London, The Tavistock Clinic, or Guy's hospital Department of Psychiatric Medicine.

1. See "Post Graduate Training in Educational and Clinical Psychology" the report of a working party, the Committee of Professional Psychologists (Mental Health) English Division, published in the *Bulletin* of the British Psychological Society, January 1955.

2. The recommendation of the above working party is that the training period should be extended to two years; the second of which should stress the aspect of "in-service training".

The Department of Education, the University of Birmingham, has since 1948 instituted (at the Remedial Education Centre) a training course for educational psychologists, students pursuing which are recognized by the Ministry of Education as eligible for substantial training grants.

YUGOSLAVIA

Psychological services of any kind are for the most part recent and tentative developments in Yugoslavia. The earliest establish-ed, as elsewhere in Europe, were vocational guidance offices, the first of which was established in 1931 by the Chamber of Commerce and Industry in Zagreb. It ceased to function in 1948 and was reopened in 1952 under the administrative and financial direction of the people's committee of the town. In Belgrade a similar organization exists under the control of the education authorities. The third centre at Ljubljana is part of the Central Hygiene Institute of the town.

Each of these centres is staffed by psychologists who to a university training in psychology have added practical courses and experience in vocational guidance. Medical services are assured either by a full-time staff or through the school medical service. As would be expected, the major clientèle of these offices consists of children at the age of school leaving (14-15 years); however a number of university students and others following higher training courses come for advice from time to time. For the most part, children and adolescents come on their own initiative, though sometimes they are sent by their parents, by their schools, or by the workshops in which they are employ-ed. The centres work closely with the employment offices, especially in Zagreb, and consequently there are frequent cross-referrals.

Relationships between the centres and University departments of psychology, medicine and neurology are close. For example, the head of the Institute of Psychology at the University of Zagreb is also head of the vocational guidance centre, and practical and theoretical training courses are organized in common between the two departments for students who wish to become vocational guidance officers. In Belgrade, the chief psychologist of the neuropsychiatric clinic of the medical school collaborates closely in certain cases.

An idea of the work undertaken by these centres is given in the following figures: Zagreb, the largest, has an average case load of 2,500-3,200, many of whom are children who come for simple information and advice and are not psychologically examined. Ljubljana has an annual load of about 500, but tested a further 1,200 pupils in secondary schools as basis for standardizing certain measures. The Belgrade centre in 1953 saw 660 children of whom 220 were psychologically examined, and at the same time tested many more for research purposes.

Because of the needs which exist, the centres frequently have to undertake tasks not strictly within their province. For example the Zagreb centre, as well as the vocational guidance of school leavers, gives a service to university students and even to adults seeking change of employment. It also undertakes vocational selection for industry. Moreover it fulfils certain psychological functions of guidance for children who are failing in school, for the subnormal, and for children with personality and behaviour problems. As other psychological services develop, it is expected that these marginal activities of the vocational guidance services will diminish.

In the Republic of Slovenia, at Maribor and at Ljubljana, there are two centres of educational guidance. These centres, the first of which has existed for several years and the second just been set up, are concerned particularly with the problems of abandoned and predelinquent adolescents.

In Zagreb there is a service concerned with mentally subnormal children of pre-school age and in 1950 the city set up a mental health unit concerned originally mainly with the prevention and treatment of alcoholism. This unit has recently developed a special service for children which fulfils many of the functions of a child guidance clinic and which treats some six to eight children daily, referred by schools, the school health and social services or by the parents themselves. The service collaborates closely with the vocational guidance service, the children's homes and the schools. In addition, it organizes public lectures, and courses for teachers and parents on mental hygiene topics. It has begun also to issue a journal. A similar centre is projected for Belgrade under the health authorities.

A beginning has also been made with a school psychological service by the appointment to the schools of Belgrade of an educational psychologist. His first task is the detection and diagnosis of mentally subnormal children for placement in special classes and a check upon placements already made. The recently formed Societies of Psychologists which are to be found in some at least of the republics are studying carefully both the structure of future services and the training and qualifications of psychologists. The current idea is that, as well as full-time educational psychologists who would form part of the Educational Council of the town, there should be specially trained teachers in each school who, whilst they would continue to do some teaching, could undertake the wider tasks of guidance of their own and their colleagues' pupils.

The difficulty in Yugoslavia, as elsewhere, resides in the lack of adequately standardized psychological instruments and techniques for the examination and guidance of school children. This in turn reflects the need for research workers in the psychological and educational fields, and of fully trained psychologists. Psychology for nearly thirty years has been an independent university discipline; but, outside the academic world, there have been few chances of employment in the vocational guidance centres. Hence trained and experienced psychologists are lacking to man the services or to develop the practical training which will meet the needs now very clearly seen.

PART III

REPORT OF AN EXPERT STUDY GROUP ON PSYCHOLOGICAL SERVICES FOR SCHOOLS AND OTHER EDUCATIONAL INSTITUTIONS[1]

THE CONTEMPORARY PROBLEM

Compulsory education has brought into the school, children from all types of social background and of all varieties and levels of ability. Thus the teacher is faced with the problem of individual differences in its most acute form. Our increasing knowledge of human psychological growth emphasizes not merely the uniqueness of each child, but a hitherto unsuspected range of interrelationships between a child's capacity to learn, the effects upon him of his experiences inside and outside the classroom and in his earlier life, and the pressures to which he is subjected by his whole social environment.

On the other hand the school has the social function, delegated to it by society, of preparing each child to participate in and contribute to his society as fully as his innate endowment permits. The core problem is that of reconciling this essential, normative preparation with the needs and rate of growth of the individual. Moreover this reconciliation has, in practice, to be made within the framework of the relatively large class, the group of thirty, forty or even more children under the care of one teacher.

As the child grows older, while there is a process of assimilation brought about by the greater uniformity of school experience, there is also an increasing differentiation of capacities, aptitudes, tastes and interests which in fact widens the range of differences between individuals. This is recognized in educational organization by offering an increasing choice between alternative studies within any school and by the choice between schools of different types. Later still, the complex economic and

1. Convened by the Unesco Institute for Education, Hamburg, from 5-10 April, 1954. For a list of the participants see p. 148.

99

industrial organization of society itself opens an even wider variety of occupations each with its particular satisfactions and each making its special demands.

Thus the school is faced with two main and closely interlocking methodological tasks, fundamental to its principal objects of aiding each child to develop fully and at the same time to become dynamically adapted to society. The first of these is to individualize methods and curricula so as to make the maximum allowance for differential rates and kinds of development among its pupils. The second is that of helping each child to choose from among the many alternatives offered, those which offer him the best chance of full personal growth.

These are not new problems; but before the turn of the present century at least, the choice of studies, of schools and of jobs was more restricted and society had evolved rough and ready methods of guidance between such alternatives as existed. For the contemporary school the problem is acute: social changes, changes in our educational philosophy and theory and an increasing awareness of difficulties, dictate an organized attempt to bring a solution by all the means at our disposal. Such an attempt, which must inevitably rely on new specializations of function, carries with it the danger that the traditional responsibilities of the teacher, of the family, and of society itself, may be in some sort undermined; or at least, that they may be shelved and thrown solely on to the expert. Such a tendency is already manifesting itself in other fields, particularly that of social welfare. Thus while underlining the need for skilled guidance for all children, this committee is of the opinion that the dangers inherent in such guidance should be recognized and guarded against. Nevertheless the legitimate responsibilities of parents and teachers are not protected by a refusal to use to the full the insights provided by the science of child psychology or by a rejection of the whole idea of experimentation cautiously undertaken. The problem to be solved is that of bringing school, parents and psychologist into effective partnership. This in turn will depend largely upon the tact and skill of the expert himself, his respect for the parents and the teachers,

his professional knowledge and above all upon his being trained
to put his insight freely at the disposal of others.

GUIDANCE

Guidance between educational alternatives cannot however be
left to rule of thumb. Because of its implications for the whole
future of a child, it demands the fullest use of the techniques
and knowledge provided by the developing science of educational psychology, and implies the close, continuous and objective
study of each pupil as a complete individual in an environment
or series of environments. Not merely must an attempt be made
to assess intellectual potentialities, special abilities, physical and
physiological capacities, but we must gain a picture of the
development of the child's personality, emotional life, attitudes
and interests. In turn this must be related to and in part explained by, his developmental history, the pressures of his
immediate family environment and of the larger milieux of his
town and the streets, of the school, of his whole status in the
human groups of which he forms part. Only by recognizing that
each child is the centre of a series of groups each influencing
him in interrelated ways and by basing our study upon his
individual psychology as well as upon his social rôles can we
aid him to make the choices which, by the organization of the
school and later of society, we offer him.

EDUCATIONAL METHODOLOGY

Such guidance, however soundly based upon the close study of
the child, will fail if the school exacts a rhythm of development
to which the individual cannot respond. In many countries
certain arbitrary standards of attainment are set by the schools;
methods have been evolved from the intuition of the adult or
from his conception of how children should learn rather than
from any close study of the ways in which children do in fact
learn. Syllabuses are, frequently, consecrated more by tradition
or inertia than by a carefully objective assessment of their

educational effectiveness. The result is that school systems present the picture of a proportion at least of children struggling along but falling ever more in arrear of the levels expected of them by teachers and administrators.

Complementary, therefore, to the concept of guidance, is the need to adapt the necessary demands made by the school to the rhythms of growth of its pupils. The individualization of materials, the study of group influences on children, the development of methods more in accordance with what is known and comes to be known of the ways in which children learn, are all necessary if human material is not to be wasted and if individual human beings are not to be warped or destroyed by their education. The administration, organization, methods and curricula of our schools are not ideal. They are based largely upon assumptions which have never been tested in the light of our knowledge of child development or upon pseudo-psychological conceptions of mental faculties, mental discipline and the transfer of training which are known to be fallacious. Thus while children should be helped to adapt happily to things as they are, psychological and educational research should be directed to an amelioration of those conditions, often outside the control of the individual teacher or school, which frequently are the true causes of children's difficulties.

EXCEPTIONAL CHILDREN

A third main problem is posed by the considerable group of children who, because of physical handicap, mental subnormality, sensory defect, severe emotional or personality deviation or disturbance and the like, cannot satisfactorily be educated in the ordinary class without some form of special provision. It is important to note that for the most part such children do not form a separate group presenting clearly distinguishable characteristics implying markedly different educational needs and methods; they are, rather, pupils who have in a more marked form, difficulties similar to those which arise (and pass away) in the personal and educational development of most children at some stage of their career. The more adequately the school is organized to cater for individual differences, the smaller becomes the proportion of children to whom it cannot adapt itself. Nevertheless however organized, and certainly with classes of thirty or more children, the ordinary primary or secondary school cannot, in justice to its more normal pupils, accept any great proportion of those who diverge markedly from the norm. Severely handicapped children are usually detected early and easily; the milder cases of sensory defect, of mental subnormality, of specific disability, of emotional disturbance or personality deviation only too frequently pass unnoticed until the child's whole educational and psychological growth has been jeopardized. Early detection of such difficulties not only prevents wastage and maladjustment, but enables positive measures to be taken if necessary, either within the class or by some form of individual provision, to enable the exceptional child to develop as satisfactorily as possible. Moreover if such children are early discovered and carefully supervised it will be found that many are not inevitably inferior or handicapped, but can after a period of special help be reintegrated into the normal class.

THE TEACHER AND THE PSYCHOLOGIST

These three tasks, of guidance, of research into the adaptation of methods and curricula, and of the discovery and, if need be, of the special remedial education of exceptional children, cannot normally be discharged by the teacher unaided. Neither by his training nor by his preoccupations is he equipped to stand aside from the child and from the educational process as a detached observer. Normally he does not have the knowledge of the techniques of child study nor the necessary training in psychological research methods. Moreover his main task is to educate, to be himself identified emotionally with the process of which he constitutes an essential factor. Thus while the teacher at all stages is and should be closely involved, he needs the assistance of the specialist in psychology. He should be helped to see the problems of the class room and the broader problems of education through the eyes of psychology, drawing from the accumulating store of psychological knowledge and research, new insights into the children he teaches and the methods he employs without however relinquishing his ultimate responsibility as a teacher.

Thus a primary function of the specialist in educational psychology is that of consultant to the teacher and to the school. Situations arise however, where the teacher or school staff are unable to accept a full responsibility for an individual problem child without injustice to the rest of the class; or, for example, a retarded pupil may need a more intensive examination, more attention or special remedial training, than the teacher is able to give. Hence specialist remedial and psychological services should be accessible to the schools, either to give expert assistance, or, in a minority of instances, temporarily to take over responsibility.

APPLIED EDUCATIONAL PSYCHOLOGY

It is clear that if psychology is to be of service to the schools in the ways outlined above, it must begin from the problems as they are met, not in the laboratory or in the clinic, but in the classroom and the whole life of the school. Effectively to do this however the psychologist must himself have profound insight into the life of the schools, into the educational process, and into the preoccupations, difficulties and professional skills of the teacher. Only on the basis of such a common professional understanding can an effective relationship be built up between teachers and psychologists so that each may, without usurping the function of the other, jointly study a particular child or a specific classroom difficulty. Without such a common understanding, the teacher is likely to reject the suggestions of the psychologist as impractical or, alternatively, to find his professional responsibilities undermined.

Thus it will be found later in this report that a principal recommendation of this committee is that school psychologists should normally be recruited from among experienced and trained teachers who shew aptitude for this difficult and exacting task. This is not proposed as an invariable rule. The crucial thing however is that whoever works with the teachers should have a sufficient practical insight into school conditions for effective co-operation. On the other hand, the committee wishes to underline the importance of the study of educational psychology and child development both in the basic professional courses for intending teachers and in further training for those who have already had classroom experience. Only on such a basis will the team work between teacher and psychologist, between schools and the psychological services develop and the disciplines of education and psychology become integrated for the benefit of all children.

CONTACT WITH THE HOME

In recent years it has come to be more and more clearly realized that a child's progress in school is intimately affected by his family life. In a stable society where family and school represent much the same values, and where their complementary functions rest upon an undisturbed basis of custom, there is probably little need for consultation. Contemporary society is in a stage of rapid change; and many parents are uncertain in their handling of their children and unguided by a healthy tradition. Moreover, universal education brings into the same classroom children from very different family environments. Thus there is a great and increasing need for home and school to co-operate in the education of children; and in a great number of cases parents need guidance and even skilled aid in the upbringing of children.

A recognition of this need has resulted in the development of various forms of parent-teacher co-operation, of parent education and the like, as well as of more specific attempts at consultative or advisory services to parents when particular decisions as to the child's future have to be made. Periodic general meetings of parents, working groups concerned with matters which touch the school at some point, visits to parents who do not attend such meetings, are all likely to facilitate contact and to bring home and school to a common under-standing.

Such contact with the parents is of great value to teachers themselves, giving them often both a greater knowledge of children and a deeper insight into particular pupils and their needs. Extreme specialisation, common at the secondary stage renders it difficult however for teachers to make genuine contacts either with individual children or their parents: the teacher who has hundreds of pupils may not even know them all by name, still less exercise a personal influence over them or have any knowledge of their family circumstances. Hence at least the head of the school, the form master or mistress or counsellor must maintain some form of personal contact with parents and be accessible to those who wish to discuss with him particular problems of their child's education.

To such co-operation the psychologist has a general contri-bution to make from his knowledge of child development. Particular situations involving individual children demand something more than this. Whenever a child is shewing signs of educational, social, or personal maladjustment, a detailed study of his home circumstances becomes essential. It often happens that the principal remedial measure to be taken is one, not of directly helping the child, but of changing the atti-tudes of the family towards him. Similarly the improvement shewn by a disturbed child during his period at a residential school may disappear when he has returned to the milieu which was a basic or contributory cause of his difficulties.

In such cases, contact with the home is a delicate matter requiring skills and insight which usually come only from a specialized training. Parents are likely to resent or reject en-quiries from teachers with whom their children are in daily contact; still less is the school able to undertake the continuous help and advice to parents that may be necessary in certain cases. Recourse to some outside service then becomes essential. If the school psychological service is adequately staffed, it normally would undertake such work or, where the maladjustment is severe, refer the case to a psychiatric clinic.

It is necessary to insist here upon an essential difference in function between the psychologist or social worker on the one hand and the member of a school teaching staff who co-operates generally with parents or gives help in the case of a particular child. By his training the teacher is an educator involved professionally in the success or failure of his pupils and should be the adviser on educational matters. The psychologist or social worker is trained to study objectively both the home and the school environments of the child and to interpret the one to the other. In many cases he will be called upon tactfully to help both to change in their methods and attitudes towards a particular child.

SPECIFIC FUNCTIONS OF A PSYCHOLOGICAL SERVICE AT VARIOUS STAGES IN EDUCATION

It is clear from the foregoing that the contribution of psychology to education is likely to be most effective if it is pervasive and integrated in the life and atmosphere of the schools, enabling the educator to attain his aims in harmony with the growth needs of each pupil. This is largely to be achieved through encouraging among all who have to do with children, an increasing sensitivity to the importance of good personal relationships. Nevertheless differentiation of function between the teacher and the psychologist is often essential. We may therefore briefly discuss those particular problems and situations in education for which some kind of specialized service is necessary.

THE PRE-SCHOOL AND PRIMARY SCHOOL

Pre-school institutions (Nursery schools and classes, kinder-gartens, Ecoles maternelles, Jardins d'Enfants) and Primary schools, in fulfilling their general task of socializing children assuring their emotional and personal growth and helping them to develop certain fundamental intellectual techniques, are brought face to face with difficulties inherent either in the rhythms of child development or in educational organization; or, as is more usual, in the combination of both. These may be summarily listed as follows:

a) *Problems of Transition:*   Most educational systems impose an age at which the child must begin school. Hence the general task of helping young children to achieve a satisfactory adaptation to a new environment is complicated by different levels of intellectual and emotional maturity which will be found in any miscellaneous group of five, six or seven year olds. Transition from home to school poses specific problems of the emotional 'weaning' and socialization of children. Later, transitions from class to class and from school to school, though effected without obvious difficulty by most children, give considerable trouble to some.

b) *Curricula and Method:*   In the primary stage, the question of guidance between alternative studies hardly arises except towards the end. All children however have to acquire certain basic intellectual techniques and a certain minimum knowledge. While this is achieved more or less effectively by the majority, there is a more considerable proportion than is usually thought —it may be as high as one in four or five children—who experience undue difficulty and for whom temporary or permanent modification of method is essential, coupled frequently with some direct assistance to the home.

c) *Home-School Co-operation:*   Apart from general, continuous and informal co-operation between teacher and parent, there are specific occasions on which contact must be as close as possible and where the family may need skilled outside help. Such are, for example, the early months of a child's school career, the time at which choice of secondary education is to be considered and whenever the child experiences continuing difficulty of educational or personal adjustment.

d) *The Discovery, Examination and Special Education of Children with Intellectual, Social, Emotional or Physical Handicaps:* The early discovery of children who are in any way handicapped, and the accurate evaluation of their needs and possibilities is an essential step towards helping them to make the most of their capacities. Individual remedial or therapeutic work, special educational methods, grouping in appropriate schools or classes is a task outside the competence of the teacher unless he has been specially trained for it.

Thus a specialized service might be expected to undertake the following tasks:

(i) Close collaboration with the teacher in the study and recording of the development of all children, and in particular in the systematic observation of individuals or of groups betraying difficulties of adjustment;

(ii) the discovery and detailed psychological and educational examination of children with physical or mental handicaps, and the suggestion and undertaking of appropriate measures, remedial or therapeutic, as seems necessary;

(iii) close collaboration with the families of problem children, with special schools or classes, or with outside services which may undertake treatment;

(iv) the propagation, in practical form, of notions of child development among teachers and parents;

(v) collaboration, through advice, through the initiation of research or through direct research assistance to teachers, in the improvement of curricula and methods, both generally and for special groups of children.

(vi) collaboration with the school medical service especially as concerns physically and mentally handicapped and problem children.

THE SECONDARY STAGE

a) *Special Needs of the Period.* Two general considerations justify the provision of psychological services designed to help children at school during their pre-adolescent and adolescent years.

In the first place, in the more developed countries where primary schooling leads to some form of secondary education for all children, the proportion who fail in their school work is very large, and roughly the same in different countries. But, since school attendance has become obligatory beyond the early primary level, it can no longer be said only that the child should adapt himself to the exigencies of the school; the school also should be adjusted to its pupils.

In the second place, certain aspects of contemporary social and economic development, which are likely to give rise to emotional tensions and so produce maladjustments, affect the child more particularly during the period of adolescence: the decrease in the economic and social importance of the family and the fact that it is not so closely knit a unit as in the past, tend to increase the number of difficulties between children and their parents; the growing complexity of society makes the achievement of economic independence more difficult; and these disturbing influences are magnified in the industrial, urban communities which are becoming ever commoner. The school cannot dissociate itself from these emotional problems because they are one of the important reasons why so many children fail to benefit from the education it provides; and the economic and social progress of society depends on the success with which the oncoming generation is educated.

Thus, in addition to tasks very similar to those described in the section dealing with the primary school, a psychological service for children in secondary schools must undertake to provide the best possible guidance between courses of study; and to help adolescents who are having difficulty in resolving their personal problems.

b) *The problem of Guidance:* When primary education is finished, the range of possibilities for pupils is considerably widened and diversified so that the problem of educational guidance arises in an acute form. Secondary education demands of the child mental activities of a somewhat different type from those required in the primary school, in particular when he begins to learn the abstract subjects. Moreover, he comes into contact with teachers who know him much less intimately, spend less time with him, and leave more responsibility to him for the organisation of his own work.

Neither success in the primary school nor objective testing at entry have, in themselves, sufficient prognostic value to serve as the sole basis for later guidance. This committee strongly recommends therefore that the early years of secondary education should be planned to allow continuous and progressive guidance of the pupils. At this stage curricula might include as well as the revision of the basic primary school subjects, an initial and active experience of a range of subjects which would permit the pupils' tastes and aptitudes to manifest themselves: some verbal and abstract studies such as a more systematic study of the mother tongue and the first steps in algebra; some essentially practical and creative courses, like manual work, craftwork, geometrical or technical drawing; some artistic activities; and some involving other forms of self-expression. These introductory classes should be small in order to permit an easy transition from the primary school atmosphere and the teachers should be chosen for those teaching abilities and psychological traits which are particularly necessary for this special task.

It would seem desirable to continue such a period of orientation at least until such time as the diversity of interests is abundantly clear—that is, up to 14 or 15 years of age. In any case, at least the first post-primary year should be the same in content, though not necessarily in level of difficulty, for all pupils. Thereafter, curricula should be specialized only gradually and progressively so that those pupils whose special aptitudes appear late may transfer from one type of course to another if necessary.

The problem of orientation is not however entirely resolved by these more flexible arrangements. The capacities which become dominant during adolescence are differentiating factors each of which may emerge and develop at a different time; moreover, the emotional effects of enlarged social experience at this age are another factor making for temporary or permanent variation in interests. And the progressive specialisation in secondary education will necessitate fresh groupings almost every year.

Clearly throughout this period of orientation and progressive specialisation, the psychological service should follow the development and progress of the children, aiding teacher, child and parent to come to decisions which are realistically based on a full appraisal of all the factors involved. It is only by continuous, skilled and *unobtrusive* supervision throughout his secondary education that little by little the pupil will find the most suitable course with the fewest of those frustrations and disappointments likely to interfere with the development of a well-balanced personality.

c) *Personal Problems:* In many contemporary schools, teachers are concerned primarily with the quality and results of their own teaching. They do not consider themselves called upon to understand and allow for the out-of-school lives and the emotional development of their pupils. This lack of interest in wider questions has sometimes been explained by the pressure of work; it is doubtful, however, whether merely lightening the teaching programme would suffice in itself to change the traditional attitude.

Psychological services thus may fulfil a double function: that of screening out, examining, and if necessary treating maladjusted children; and that of contributing through case discussion and other means, to a change in teachers' attitudes and to helping them to increase their insight into the relation between a child's emotional life and his school work. Experience demonstrates that, where a good relationship between teacher and psychologist is developed, the school can not only become a happier place for most children but make a contribution to the prevention of maladjustment and delinquency. Once the problems have been discovered, the school psychologist himself may undertake remedial measures or in cases requiring prolonged examination or treatment, may call in the Child Psychiatric Clinic or some other specialized service. The school psychological service however must not lose contact with the child.

TECHNICAL AND PRE-VOCATIONAL EDUCATION

In technical, pre-vocational and multilateral schools there is an even greater necessity for continuous guidance between educational alternatives and for skilled handling of personal difficulties and problems. In the schools with a more markedly occupational bias, however, educational and vocational guidance should be earlier and more intimately associated. Moreover, in guiding pupils who will ultimately be integrated in commerce or in industry, physical factors and aptitudes and medical contra-indications may be of more importance than they are for those whose education is preparing them for an academic career. In most countries a considerable democratization of education has taken place; but it remains true that the academic secondary course preponderantly attracts those whose socio-economic circumstances are good. Technical, trade, and vocational schools on the contrary, tend to have a higher proportion of pupils from relatively unfavourable socio-economic milieux. Consequently contact with and help to the families as well as aid to individual adolescents assume an even greater importance.

There rests a further series of problems peculiar to the size of many such schools and their tendency to offer a larger and larger variety of courses. The big multilateral school may have many parallel classes corresponding in part to differences in ability of the pupils and in part to differences in choice of options. In any one grade, there may be as many as ten or more class units. The distribution of pupils among these so that individual needs are not neglected and at the same time so that the range of ability in any one class is not too wide, can only be based upon an objective study of the capacities, aptitudes and interests of the pupils. Examinations too, whether for promotion from class to class or at the end of studies, raise the problems of objectivity, prognostic value, and equivalence. The educational psychologist trained in research methods and well aware of the limitations and possibilities of tests and measures is an essential collaborator with the teacher in this field.

TRANSITION FROM SCHOOL TO WORKING LIFE. RELATIONS BE-TWEEN PSYCHOLOGICAL SERVICES AND VOCATIONAL GUIDANCE

It is necessary in this connection to clear up an ambiguity which may arise in the use of the word guidance (orientation) in two connections, an ambiguity which sometimes leads to regrettable confusions.

A *vocational guidance* service is concerned with the choice of employment, may not have responsibility for putting into practice the advice it gives, and uses the results of psychological testing along with other types of data such as job analysis and information as to the state of the labour market.

A *school psychological service* can be fully effective only to the extent to which it is integrated with the school; the guidance it offers depends on psychological information of very various kinds and it is concerned with helping children whose development it follows closely.

a) *Guidance a Continuous Process:*   Clearly vocational guidance cannot be effective if it takes the form of a snapshot intervention at the end of the child's school career and on the threshold of working life. To a considerable degree educational guidance, particularly at the secondary stage, is itself a form of vocational guidance by the implications which the choice of studies has for a subsequent widening or narrowing of the field of vocational choice. The expert committee would not wish to suggest that educational guidance should be based upon vocational considerations; the main preoccupation should be that of guiding the child's general personal and educational development. However, in the later stages of compulsory schooling or in the final years of the secondary school the choice of a career becomes increasingly important psychologically to young people and the school psychological service must enter into a closer functional relationship with vocational guidance services. Ideally, there should be a convergence between the services giving educational guidance, and those concerned with the vocational field.

How this is to be brought about will depend upon factors peculiar to the educational systems of different countries. A truly comprehensive service would—though with differences of personnel and of emphasis—follow a child from his entry to school until he is satisfactorily integrated into working life. Where, however, as is not unusual, school psychological services and vocational guidance services depend on different ministries and are financed from different sections of the budget, then means must be found, not merely to effect an interchange of information at a relatively late stage in the child's school career or even after it is over, but to bring about a continuous working co-operation throughout at least the second half of post-primary education.

Vocational guidance services can usefully be called in to tell pupils something about the chief local occupations and draw their attention to those which have vacancies or offer chances for advancement. On the other hand, the work of the vocational guidance services can be given a more secure basis by making use of some of the information available from the school psychological service, in particular that built up by the school staff and the psychologist and contained in the school record card. According to local circumstances, and in particular to the training and qualification of its staff, the one service or the other would carry out any necessary supplementary examination and study of the aptitudes, interests and personality of the adolescents concerned.

A more thorough understanding of each other's work and specialisation will enable the psychologist and vocational guidance officer to avoid duplication of effort. And, in the final phase when children and parents have to decide upon choice of occupation or of vocational training the two services should be present in conference, at least for the difficult cases.

b) *Difficulties of entry to the Workshop:* Guidance as to choice of occupation is not however sufficient to ensure a smooth transition from school to working life. Statistical studies show for example that, especially among young workers who have not had the transitional experience of a vocational school or apprenticeship, a high proportion make many changes of job before they settle down more or less satisfactorily. Nevertheless, most young people are glad to leave school, moved by the hope of achieving greater independence or status, by the wish for the adventure of adult life, or sometimes simply by a dislike of school where they have been bored or disappointed.

Children are however apt to experience the change as unexpectedly abrupt and bewildering. Their school has essentially treated them as individuals whose welfare was a first consideration. The workshop, they find, is concerned with an impersonal and often abstract thing, production; they feel themselves to be merely cogs in the machine. Often they find little help from the adult workers or foremen, who are themselves in a similar situation. In short, especially among the least qualified, the impression that they are being used for secondary tasks which have no glamour, disappoints their hope of acquiring adult prestige rapidly. This is one at least of the sources of states of tension which show themselves either by manifestations of discouragement, or by a negativistic attitude—blustering or waggish—or by indifference and lack of interest in work. And the search for noisy or narcotic distractions is often only a compensation for basic lack of satisfaction in work.

It can safely be said that nowhere as yet has a solution to these and similar problems of transition been satisfactorily found; nor indeed are we fully aware of all the factors, social, psychological and economic, which tend towards adjustment or maladjustment to work. Nevertheless, much could and should be done through apprenticeship centres, through factory welfare services, through part-time day release classes, technical colleges, and the like, and through interesting foremen and senior workers in the adolescent, to avoid the waste, frustration and even serious disturbance which result from a system of laissez-faire.

In such an effort, a comprehensive psychological service containing within itself or collaborating with services of vocational guidance and advice, and working in close co-operation with centres of extended eduation, apprenticeship schemes, community social services, trade unions and factory managements could play a dynamic rôle. This committee hopes that in the near future carefully planned experiments of various kinds will be undertaken by industry in co-operation with the available services and aimed not only at an empirical solution of the many problems that beset the young worker at the outset of his career but also at a clearer appreciation of the psychological and social pressures which may operate to produce a progressive dulling of the capacity actively to enjoy work and leisure.

GUIDANCE AND COUNSELLING SERVICES AT THE UNIVERSITY

The proportion of university students who experience severe psychological difficulty—either in the first year of their studies or later—seems to have increased to disquieting proportions. Apart from the toll of personal frustration and failure which this entails, it represents a grave loss to the community as a whole and is a sufficient justification for efforts to organize effective guidance services in institutions of higher education.

A word may be said as to the causes of this increased incidence of mental disturbance among university students. Since the early twenties at least there has been a steady increase in the number of students attending universities and other institutions of higher education. This has inevitably meant a democratization of recruitment. Many, if not the majority, of students now come from families of modest means and suffer from the strain of feeling that they must, at all costs, succeed vocationally. At the same time they may receive little support and understanding from a family which, however well intentioned, has had no prior experience of what higher studies mean. Another factor of uncertainty lies in the inability of the student (a situation also found at the secondary level) to orient himself among the ever-increasing number of specialized courses at a time when he is still ignorant of the realities of the profession towards which his studies are leading him.

The growing complexity of technical, economic, social and administrative activity moreover makes satisfactory vocational guidance and entry into employment more difficult. In former times most students found entry to a profession relatively easy after completing their university courses. Nowadays the university qualification or even the technical diploma does not guarantee employment; and worry on this account may already be affecting the student during his course of study. Political insecurity and the uprooting of populations is another source of anxiety; in certain countries, gifted young people, in addition to the effort demanded by their studies and the misery of having had to leave their native country, have to earn their living. These factors lead to a kind of ambivalent attitude which is not always favourable to well-balanced intellectual development: the need for rapid success seems to demand narrow specialisation, but leaves unsatisfied the desire to profit from the cultural riches offered by University life.

Difficulties may have begun moreover before the end of the secondary school course, with the tension and often the overwork experienced by students in those countries where secondary studies end with external or internal examinations, on the results of which depend any chances of receiving higher education. Nor is the transition itself easy from the more or less regimented life of the school to the freer and more responsible atmosphere of the University. Certainly in the long run it may well be a very useful experience, conducive to personal development, for the student to have to organise his own life and develop a method of work. But at the cost of how many checks and wasted efforts is this experience acquired by those fortunate ones who succeed in passing the danger-points without serious accidents?

It is clearly important that schools and universities should find some solution to those problems and it seems at the present time that a number of convergent measures is better than any single method. These it is suggested should be as follows:

(i) Educational guidance must be continued up to the end of the secondary course, and into the first university year at least. Such guidance is greatly facilitated where school and university co-operate to provide, for example, visits in the final school year to special laboratories or institutions, lecture courses by specialists on the opportunities offered by Universities, what they lead to, and on other aspects of university life. A further valuable measure is the setting up of University Offices of information and documentation linked both with the schools and with employment services. Such centres, however, need the collaboration of the professions and adequate and up-to-date statistical services in order to give a real picture of the activities and current conditions in the possible professions to which the various courses may lead.

(ii) As at the beginning of the secondary school course, so at the outset of higher studies, a course of orientation should help the students to make the transition from secondary school to university. In certain countries the highest form in the secondary school is organised with this aim in view; the instruction, rather than attempting to cover an overloaded programme superficially, is concentrated on a thorough study of a few typical subjects, and a considerable part of the timetable is reserved for pupils to work up the material themselves. When economic conditions permit, it seems desirable that such a course of orientation should be given at the beginning of higher education, provided that University teachers do not, on the pretext of providing general culture, use the time at their disposal to extend their own courses. The objective would be to concentrate the attention of the pupils on the methods peculiar to the disciplines which they wish to follow so that they may see their way more clearly. At the same time, as well as contributing to general culture, such an orientation period would allow both an informed choice of later specialisation and an appraisal of the vocational field.

(iii) In many Universities there are supervisory services intended to help the students during their first years. Sometimes this is by the tutorial system whereby students are attached to a member of staff who acts as supervisor of studies and may, if he is humanly able to do so, act also as a guide, philosopher, and friend to his charges. Sometimes tutorial responsibility is exercised by university graduates in the town, who stand in *loco parentis* to a student coming from the same region or belonging to the same social class. More often, it is students in their later years who, at the request of their associations, take responsibility for younger students. This system often leads to the spontaneous organisation of discussion groups among the students, where personal problems are broached with more complete freedom.

(iv) There remains however a core of problems for which

these solutions do not suffice, and which demand more skill and insight than can reasonably be expected of university teachers preoccupied with academic specialities. For these the most efficient solution is likely to be the provision of a complete student guidance service. Such a service which might co-operate with or even form a part of the student health service, would need one or more full time counsellors and should be able to draw upon the part-time assistance of colleagues with special qualifications in departments of psychology, medicine and social science. For those students who pursue courses in Education, Psychology, or other of the Social Sciences, much can be done also through their actual courses in Psychology, if some at least of these take as their point of departure, an examination of the personal problems actually arising in the life of the students. This however is desirable only if the teachers have themselves a sufficient practical training in psychology and can understand and control the emotions and anxieties which such a direct approach may unleash.

TEACHER TRAINING

A word should be said specially concerning the training and further training of teachers. Prospective teachers have the same needs as University students generally and the same considerations apply. There are however, in addition, three further rôles which the science of educational psychology should increasingly fulfil, in part at least through applied services.

It is recognized that in the educational development of the children he teaches, the personality of the teacher plays a large part. In spite therefore of the shortage of candidates for training as teachers, many countries are experimenting with methods of selection which at least will exclude those who for various personality reasons, are unsuitable for the profession. Teacher training departments, University centres of research, and the psychological services, might well collaborate closely in research to define methods and criteria of selection and in their application and follow-up.

It will be obvious, from what has earlier been said, that a psychological service for schools cannot function adequately without the informed co-operation of the teachers. The foundation for this must be laid in the years of basic training when the student should not merely receive theoretical and practical instruction in educational psychology but should also, if possible, be brought into contact with a functioning service. This facilitates later co-operation and gives reality to courses which only too often students find dull and irrelevant. It is indeed probable that the psychologist in daily contact with problems of the social and educational development of children through participation in a school psychological service, is the person best situated to aid training institutions in giving the future teacher a sound insight into child development.

The third task in which the psychological services should co-operate is that of the further training of experienced teachers. We have already stressed the value of discussion between teacher and psychologist of particular problem children or of particular aspects of educational method. This is a continuing process of in-service training which will operate to the mutual advantage of teacher and psychologist. There however remains the whole field of short courses and of more extended specialized training, especially for those teachers who will undertake remedial work or work in schools or classes dealing with mentally or physically handicapped children. Here again the psychological service from its intimate contact with the practicalities of education and with social and psychological factors outside the usual range of the class teacher's preoccupations, has a major part to play.

THE SCOPE AND FUNCTIONS OF A SCHOOL PSYCHOLOGICAL SERVICE

COMPREHENSIVENESS

In no country in Europe have services been developed to the point where all the needs, outlined in the first two sections of this report, are fully and adequately met. The central problems of organization are those of seeing to it on the one hand that the technical help of psychology is at the daily service of the teacher without usurping his proper functions and on the other that specialized treatment of the appropriate kind is available when it is needed. Hence a school psychological service has advisory, remedial and co-ordinating functions and should make the bridge between the schools and all the other services, social and medical, which directly or indirectly contribute to the healthy, personal, educational and social growth of children. It should also aim at ensuring that all the needs are covered adequately at all stages of growth from the pre-school period to integration into adult working life.

THE SIZE OF THE POPULATION TO BE SERVED

A service so conceived will have need of different types of worker with different patterns of experience and qualification—but essential to it is the educational psychologist in intimate daily contact with the schools, and with children at all stages in their school career. The provision of enough fully trained and competent psychologists however is probably a dream for the future. Neither the supply of suitable candidates for the profession nor the present facilities for training is adequate to meet the foreseeable demands even of the most modest kind. The expert group moreover is firmly of the opinion that it is better to have too few psychologists of high quality than to multiply those whose lack of theoretical training or whose inadequate experience leads them into serious mistakes and undermines the effectiveness of the service given.

The educational guidance of the school child, which has been insisted upon earlier as a vital task, is not one that can be discharged by a snap judgement or even by a day or two of testing. It is a matter for continuous and careful observation supplemented, in those cases where the child has no declared aptitudes or where particular difficulties arise, by a more specialized study. As such, in addition to the services of a supervising psychologist, one class counsellor or specially trained teacher would be necessary for 400-500 children, and could work with a whole school staff. Where the school unit is a large one—say one to two thousand children—it is necessary to have a school psychologist and a social worker together with a teacher trained in the administration of group tests. Such a team can assure the tasks of counselling and guidance, and the more general functions of aiding the school staff to ameliorate the psychological atmosphere of the school; it can give assistance with more difficult individual cases, and screen out and undertake the treatment of those cases which require deeper, and more prolonged study.

Such a solution though desirable in many ways, is far from being generally realisable and alternative solutions have to be sought. The nature of these depends in part upon circumstances peculiar to each country and its school system and in part upon the actual type of population in question. For example, where the teachers, and especially the heads of schools, have themselves had a sound psychological training, and where an effective system of school record cards is in use, the task of guiding children between options can safely be left to the school staff, the psychological service giving its particular attention to difficult cases and generally trying to improve guidance methods for use by teachers. Similarly in rural areas where schools are small, it would be impossibly uneconomic to attempt to provide one psychologist for each school; in such circumstances the travelling psychological service operating from a number of part-time centres has been found effective.

The range and variety of services offered, the co-ordination made among the varied types of workers in one way or another entering into a psychological contact with children and with their families—district nurses, welfare workers, teachers, doctors, magistrates etc.—and the effectiveness with which the various kinds of more or less serious psychological problems met with among school populations can be tackled, does however directly depend upon the number, as well upon the quality of psychological staff available. And the number of staff required cannot be defined in terms of a case load, since the time required by an individual case may vary from an hour to as much as several days or even weeks. Hence the only practical basis of estimate for the staffing of a school psychological service, in terms of all the functions it should fulfil, is continued experience; and this experience will be dependent upon such factors as density of population, accessibility of the service, the sociological nature of the population, and the richness of the services provided. The committee does not wish to lay down hard and fast standards but experience seems to indicate that a minimum service, in an urban area presenting no special difficulties of communication or of social composition, can be assured by not fewer than two psychologists for a school population of 12,000-15,000 children. *Such a minimum implies that the teaching staff of the school are sufficiently trained themselves to assure the effective educational guidance of the majority of children*; that the facilities of a fully staffed child guidance centre are at their disposal; that adequate special school provision, remedial classes and the like are integrated with the service; and finally that close liaison is maintained with a sufficient service of vocational guidance. It is reemphasised, however, that this is a *minimum*, and not the ideal; and that, moreover, the suggestion made does not imply that it is more than an acceptable alternative to the psychologist operating within the large school unit.

THE ORGANISATION OF A SERVICE

It is not possible at the present stage to lay down organisational details of a school psychological service which would be universally applicable; it is however possible to suggest certain principles which embodied in organization, administration and finance will allow the development of a service able to meet the needs described earlier in this report. These we believe to be as follows:

a)   The service should be *comprehensive and flexible* both in organization and in staffing so that it may develop to meet the needs of the schools as they declare themselves and may be able to follow a case through to a successful conclusion;

b) *The contact with the schools should be close and intimate.*
On the personal level this will come about through the training
of the psychologist himself who would normally be recruited
from the teaching profession. Organizationally however this
contact is best secured by attaching the service directly to the
education authority, national or local.

c) *The service itself should contain the necessary specialised
units* for child guidance, remedial teaching, speech reeducation
and the like and be closely associated with special schools or
classes for various types of exceptional or handicapped children.
It should also contain or be very closely associated with vocational guidance services and with student counselling work in
higher education.

d) *It should co-operate especially over particular cases with,
but not be subordinated to, the school medical service and through
this have access to the specialised medical services as may be
necessary.*

e) *Its responsibilities should not be limited to children of compulsory school age.* Thus it should be possible for the service
to enter into co-operation with the maternal and child welfare
clinics at the one end and with factory welfare schemes for the
adolescent worker at the other.

f) A special word should be said on finance. A comprehensive
service of the type proposed in this report cannot be financed
on the basis of the number of cases treated or by differential
grants from the same or different authorities for different aspects
of the service. *The finance provided must be adequate* to enable
all aspects—the schools advisory service, the diagnostic and
treatment services as well as the numerous special calls upon the
skill and knowledge of the staff—to function as the needs make
themselves felt and with shifts of emphasis as the work develops.
In work of the kind proposed for the school psychological
service, experience repeatedly shows that a ton of prevention
costs less than an ounce of cure; and the financing of the service
should be such that the preventive aspects of its work are not
sacrificed to the need to maintain a given case load for examination and treatment in order to earn a grant. The commit-

tee strongly recommends that a global grant be made from the education budget in a category distinct from that for other services; in this way the psychological service will be enabled to function as a unity rather than as a series of differently financed and more or less separate services.

CO-ORDINATION WITH OTHER SERVICES

The educational psychologist, whether working in the school or from an external service, will normally not have the time to deal completely with all the individual difficulties which may present themselves among children. Many of the questions of method and of organization, for example, demand extensive research in which a number of classes or schools may be involved. Similarly, although the majority of difficulties arising in the course of the education of children can be solved by collaboration between psychologist, parent and teacher yet there is a core of problems which demand both more intensive study and more specialized treatment than the school psychologist may have time to give. Severe cases of maladjustment arising from conditions internal to the pupil, or in his home life, for example, may demand special remedial action, psychotherapy or a radical change in the child's environment. The psychologist must be able to refer such cases to the specialist services of a child guidance centre, a psychiatric unit or medico-educational institute either for a more thorough study or for remedial action. Many problems of retardation among children of all levels of ability also require special study and special remedial methods which may involve the removal, temporarily at all events, of the child from his normal class, and his placement in a remedial or coaching group. Similarly University departments of research or special research institutions should provide the facilities for the basic research in child development and educational method necessary for the progressive adaptation of the school to the child and the child to the school. Clearly too the psychologist should have access to the school medical service and to the welfare and social services of the community.

Most European countries are developing a considerable variety of special provision for children who cannot be educated in the ordinary schools though none has sufficient as yet. The blind, the deaf, the crippled,[1] the partially sighted, the hard of hearing, children with speech defects, the mentally subnormal[2] and the severely maladjusted or delinquent are more or less adequately provided for. Such schools or classes however should have a functional connection with the normal educational system and should have access to the school psychological services. In many instances it will be the psychologist himself who first recommends special schooling for a particular child; in others it will be the medical services; in the case of delinquents it may be the court or the probation service which recommends that children be seen by the psychological service so that appropriate educational advice can be given. In all instances, and particularly in those cases which are marginal, a close psychological supervision is necessary if the child is to profit from the special provision made for him and to be returned whenever feasible to the normal stream of education. Thus a complete service must envisage a number of specialized services with which the school psychologist should act as a link and which in the majority of cases he will co-ordinate, especially where for administrative reasons they are separately conducted and financed.

Because, however, of national or regional peculiarities of development or because of financial difficulties, the school psychological service may not contain within itself all the specialized diagnostic and treatment units which may be necessary. Moreover there are other services which from time to time are necessary and which, although they touch on the educational sphere, have their main preoccupations elsewhere.

1. See the report of the *Joint Expert Committee on the Physically Handicapped Child* (W.H.O., U.N., I.L.O., Unesco). W.H.O. Tech. Report Series No. 58. Geneva, 1952.
2. See the report of the *Joint Expert Committee on the Mentally Subnormal Child* (W.H.O., U.N., I.L.O., Unesco). W.H.O. Tech. Report Series No. 74. Geneva, 1954.

Not infrequently the services required to help any given child and his family are fragmented among a number of administrations and are financed from different budgets.

Where no co-ordination exists, wasteful overlapping is regrettably frequent. Workers from different services severally make contact with the family, give sometimes conflicting advice and make financial and administrative arrangements which may well be at variance. We may accept the rule that only one authority should be concerned principally at any one time and add that the overriding authority should be the service which takes the case in hand. In most cases which arise in school the educational psychologist is essentially at the service of the teacher. The power therefore to take action affecting the instruction and education of pupils, and the responsibility for such action, remains with the teacher and the school. If, however, the psychologist or the psychological service undertakes remedial work, then the responsibility for direction of the case must be in the hands of the service. If an outside unit—such for example as the medical service or child psychiatric clinic—is called into consultation merely, responsibility still remains with the psychological service or the school. If, however, a specialized unit undertakes treatment, then while the school psychological service will continue to maintain contact and to collaborate, direction and responsibility will pass to the specialized unit.

Even when based on such a principle, however, collaboration and integration between different services inevitably raises administrative and financial questions and problems of professional responsibility. Certain aspects of a truly comprehensive service—for example the guidance of parents of very young children—may perhaps fall within the scope of the maternal and child welfare service; others—for example that of vocational guidance and adjustment to work—may be considered as more in the field of those administrations concerned with labour problems. The core of the services for the child of school age will clearly be in the province of the education authorities. It should not however be beyond the bounds of possibility to bring about, at the administrative level, a reasonable division of financial and organisational responsibility and at the functional level a close working relationship between the services provided.

Similarly on the basis of a recognition of and respect for the different contributions which can be made by the specialisations of education, psychology, medicine and social work, it is possible for a team approach to be developed among individuals working together over particular problems. The composition of such a team, its leadership and the responsibilities of each member should vary widely with the circumstances. It may range from the relatively simple collaboration of the teacher and psychologist, to more elaborate groups, such as the child guidance clinic team of psychologist, psychiatrist and psychiatric social worker, or specially constituted groups to consider the complex problems posed by cases in which particular physical or sensory difficulties enter. In such team work it is essential that each member should contribute from his own specialized viewpoint and that the group should reach a *joint* decision based upon all the contributions. Where the decision is truly joint, questions of leadership and of the responsible discipline do not arise; where there is a conflict of opinion then it must be resolved in the way outlined earlier. The committee is however concerned to state that no considerations of inter-professional or inter-administrative rivalry should be allowed to hinder the organic use of available services for the benefit of all children: and it is sometimes of value to set up a joint committee for continuous consultation among the authorities concerned, at least in the early stages of the development of a psychological service.

STAFFING

Though the key worker in a psychological service for schools will be the educational psychologist himself, many other types of worker are required, all of whom should have some general insight into the work of the schools. Normally, for example, contact with the homes and much of the task of aiding parents will be discharged by the social worker or, in part, by the school welfare officer. Remedial education for individual failing children or the special education necessary for some types of disturbed, mentally or physically handicapped children will be undertaken by teachers specially trained for the tasks. So too where teachers with a sufficient complement of psychological training are available, they may well be called upon to act as class counsellors, to aid with general educational guidance and in some instances to conduct the first examinations of children presenting problems of educational and personal development. In view of the high level of training and of professional responsibility required of the educational psychologist, efforts should be made to increase the number of those who can, under his supervision, undertake many of the time-consuming and more or less routine tasks which form the main load of a service, leaving him with time and energy free to concentrate upon these problems for which his training specially fits him.

The specialized services of vocational guidance, child guidance, educational and psychological research, have need of psychologists with an emphasis of training different from that required for direct contact with the schools and will call upon other specialities, such as psychiatry, pediatrics, statistics, industrial psychology and social work. It would be inappropriate in this report to enter into details of the training and functions of such workers. The Committee however wishes to point out that, in so far as the staff of these services come into contact with children of school age or with educational problems they too need to have more adequate knowledge of schools than is simply derived from once having been educated.

In certain cases the school psychologist may be expected to work both in the school and in the specialized unit such as the child psychiatric clinic or vocational guidance team. In others he may be required to interpret to colleagues from other disciplines the educational considerations of which account has to be taken in dealing with individual children. Such co-operation is greatly facilitated where the psychologist himself through his training and his work is given an insight into the activities of other professions and where the training of the medical and social work personnel concerned includes a genuine study of education and psychology. It is to be hoped that in the not too distant future the training and further training of all those professions directly concerned with children and adolescents of school age, will contain certain common studies and will in part be undertaken conjointly. In this way the basis of team work will be laid and differentiation of function will not lead either to rivalry or to wasteful overlapping.

RESEARCH

The practical functioning service has its roots in and should draw its life blood from continuous association with Universities and with special institutes of educational and psychological research. There should be a constant interchange between the work in the field which throws up research problems and the laboratory or research team which commands the facilities for rigorous enquiry. In such a way the field psychologist and the research worker may both derive benefit and the daily service will not lag behind in the application of the findings of educational and psychological experiment. This general recommendation may be carried further. The committee holds the view that the professional training of the educational psychologist should be conducted in close association with active departments of educational and psychological research. Moreover the psychological service should be so staffed and financed that the practising psychologist has the time and is encouraged to co-operate closely with a research institute in the scientific study of the problems posed by his daily practice, at least, if not to undertake individual research work himself. Only in this way, will the full and continuous growth of the service in its technical aspects be ensured and the results of fundamental research in the various aspects of child study and education rapidly be ploughed back into practice.

Attention is however drawn by the committee to the fact that in most countries, even those in which psychological work is relatively well developed, research in the field of child study and of the psychology of education is badly underfinanced and depends for the most part upon the good will and voluntary effort of a few psychologists in universities and in existing services. Adequate research into the psychological development of children, into methods of treatment and of special education and into all the multitudinous problems which currently present themselves in the field of applied psychology, requires staff and money which organisations hard pressed by other demands cannot give. The committee urges upon the responsible authorities the need for a considerably expanded finance for research into this important field.

Basic and applied research should be complemented by a third type which in the present state of development of services is equally essential. In each country, at least one controlled pilot project of a full service should be carried out over a period of years, under research conditions and with the widest facilities for experiment in organisation, administration and staffing. Such experiments should be carefully planned to take place in typical areas presenting as many as possible of the problems to be faced. They should aim at a continuing evaluation of the effectiveness of different methods of bringing psychology into the service of the school, the value and limitations of different types of training, and of remedial methods, and should offer an ideal towards which other services elsewhere would move.

THE SELECTION, TRAINING AND PROFESSIONAL RESPONSIBILITY OF THE EDUCATIONAL PSYCHOLOGIST

THE EDUCATIONAL PSYCHOLOGIST AS THE KEY WORKER

It has been stated earlier that the educational psychologist is the key to a successful school psychological service. Properly chosen and fully trained, working either within a particular school or group of schools or from an external service in close contact with the schools, he is the most effective channel whereby knowledge of child development may be brought directly into the service of education. He can advise the teacher over the minor difficulties presented by individual children, carry out more intensive and detailed case studies, assess levels of intellectual and personal development and suggest modifications of method or programme in the light of his observations. He too is well situated both to initiate experiments in educational methodology and to pass on to his colleagues the teachers the results of research.

Working in this way as the teacher's collaborator, he is in a particularly favourable position to influence the whole life of the school by bringing the insights of psychology to bear upon its daily problems. He does not make his colleagues into psychologists; he should however, by his way of looking at particular cases and situations, bring them to see their task in the light of the developmental psychology of childhood. Similarly the psychologist either working alone or collaborating with the teacher or with the school head, can greatly assist in establishing co-operation with parents and, in special cases, with the families of those children whose school difficulties are a reflection of disturbances at home. The success which he ultimately achieves in that task, however, depends directly upon his insight into and understanding of the teacher's problems; and such insight and understanding can only rarely be developed by the psychologist who has not himself been a teacher. Therefore most countries which have developed a school psychological service now insist upon considerable teaching experience as a necessary qualification for the practice of psychology in the educational field.

The committee here wishes to reemphasize the essential difference in function and aptitude between the teacher and the educational psychologist. The main responsibility of the teacher is to educate his pupils. In doing this, his own personality is part of the educational climate in which the child learns; he builds up an affective relationship, positive or negative with the children he teaches and is himself deeply involved in the process. The psychologist must be observant, able to evaluate and understand objectively all the factors in the child and in the educational situation, without becoming himself emotionally involved to the point where his judgment is affected. It is essential that he should be able not only to understand and use the methods and techniques of his profession but to understand the human problems posed by each individual case. The psychologist not infrequently finds it necessary to draw the attention of the school to the importance of the affective relationships between pupils and teacher which may be overlooked in too exclusive a preoccupation with method. On the other hand he must see to it that the teacher does not become too immersed in the multiplicity of human relationships and thus lose control of his class.

Thus while insisting that the educational psychologist should himself have been a teacher, the committee wishes to add certain cautions. The training, experience, and professional preoccupations of the teacher are essentially different from those required by a psychologist. Moreover the qualities of personality called into play are often not the same. Thus careful selection and a thorough supplementary training are necessary; the first to ensure that the personal qualities necessary to the profession of educational psychologist are present or can be developed; and the second as the basis for effective work. The very newness of applied psychology, the relative uncertainty of many of its findings and techniques, and the wide and far reaching demands which are made upon its services, all mean that it should only be exercised by those who after a long and profound training are fully aware of its limitations. This is not to say that teachers with a complement of psychological knowledge short of the full training outlined later are not of value to the whole life of the school; it is however to insist that final responsibility for the applications of psychology to education and to individual children, should only be entrusted to those whose training is as complete as current knowledge can make it. A word too should be said about the practice in some countries of having a psychologically trained teacher or even an educational psychologist in charge of a class and at the same time acting as adviser to his colleagues on psychological problems. The committee considers that, in view of the distinction between the teaching and psychological functions, they cannot normally be exercised simultaneously and that it is inadvisable for one and the same person to be class teacher and psychologist to the same group of children.

THE FUNCTIONS OF THE SCHOOL PSYCHOLOGIST

It is not easy for all purposes and for all social and administrative situations, to define the appropriate functions of the school psychologist. These will in part depend upon the qualifications expected of those who exercise the psychological function in the schools, upon the availability of other specialists and auxiliaries, and upon the existence of specialized psychiatric and remedial services. Moreover it is in just those areas where teachers are not as well trained as they should be and where the various auxiliary services of special education, child guidance and the like do not exist that the remedial and advisory services of the educational psychologist are most necessary. Such areas, often rural districts with small schools widely spread, would find a full service difficult to institute and to finance and initially the activity of a psychologist may have to be confined to immediately urgent problems. Nevertheless, without setting priorities, the following minimal functions may be indicated as a first goal towards which any service should work.

(a) He will collaborate with the teachers in the general work of educational guidance, applying whatever standardized tests may be necessary and making thorough individual case studies of children as appropriate. The problem of guidance may be expected to arise not only at the beginning of the secondary school course but whenever a choice of studies must be made and whenever cases of children experiencing difficulty in any particular course are reconsidered;

(b) Naturally following from the above, he will be responsible for establishing in conjunction with his colleagues the teachers the cumulative individual record card for each pupil, for training teachers, if necessary, in its use, and for assisting them to maintain it as a principal document to be consulted when important decisions are to be made;

(c)   He will work with teachers, heads of schools and the inspectorate to improve educational methods and the climate of the classroom, bringing to bear upon such problems the specialized knowledge derived from research. In this connection it is important that he should have sufficient time to take part in educational research in conjunction with his colleagues or with teachers.

(d)   He will co-operate in, and if necessary, assume the major responsibility for, the examination of children with personal problems. According to the nature of the case, he will raise the question of remedial or other treatment in whatever quarter seems appropriate; with individual teachers, with the head of the school, with the social worker, school medical officer, or with outside services or organizations;

(e)   He must be responsible for liaison between all those different services concerned with the educational progress and healthy mental and emotional development of the pupils;

(f)   So far as is possible he will take part in school staff meetings, particularly when general problems of child development are to be discussed, or when individual children are considered.

SELECTION AND TRAINING OF SCHOOL PSYCHOLOGISTS

Clearly even to discharge such minimal functions effectively and with a full sense of the responsibilities which he may have to assume, the school psychologist should be carefully selected and have a training of the highest quality both theoretical and practical. The following minima seem to meet with general agreement (though far from universally realized) in those countries where psychological services are effectively functioning.

(a)   *Basic Training and Qualifications:*

   (i)   A University qualification in psychology at a high level (e.g. *Licence en psychologie*, France, or an Honours degree in Psychology, U.K.).

(ii)] A teaching diploma or other professional qualification as a teacher.

(iii) Educational experience. At least five years of teaching experience, preferably varied, should be required for those who wish to work in schools. A minimum of three years of work with normal children should be demanded of those who wish to work more particularly in the clinical field.

(b) *Selection for Professional Training:*

It may be agreed that there should be little or no selection (other than is customary for entry to other university schools) of those who wish to study psychology at the undergraduate level. It is however essential that a rigorous selection should subsequently be made of those who wish to become school psychologists. The committee agrees that the criteria should be at least as follows:

(i)   In those countries where different levels or classes of university degree exist, a high level of academic attainment (1st. or 2nd. class honours for example) should be demanded of a candidate for professional training;

(ii) The candidate should satisfy the training institution that he has a good level of capacity and has achieved a good professional adjustment in teaching or any other acceptable type of work with children;

(iii) By means of a preliminary period of at least one month devoted to observation and information, the training institution should satisfy itself that the candidate possesses the personal qualities necessary to the profession of educational psychologist, and that he is well acquainted with its demands.

To the above general criteria, of selection, training and qualification one may envisage two types of exception, which will be handled according to local conditions. The first is for those already working in the profession before the establishment of conditions of admission. Clearly, subject to the necessary professional safeguards, such workers should be confirmed in their acquired right to practise. Secondly, there are candidates with something of value to contribute but whose previous training and experience are different from those outlined above. Such cases should be considered individually on their merits with the proviso that the preliminary qualifications demanded should be equivalent in value.

It is clear that, under the conditions outlined above, educational psychologists will in the main be recruited from among those who already have some seniority in teaching or another cognate profession. Hence this committee urges administrative authorities (and in particular Ministries of Education) to take measures, by the release of staff members for professional training, and in selected cases, for the basic training as well, on full salary or aided by bursaries, to ensure that suitable candidates come forward.

(c) *Responsibility for Professional Training:*

The committee recommends that the professional training should be undertaken by a University or institution of higher learning of university status and should lead to a special diploma in Educational Psychology. The content and method of the training and the final examination however should be agreed between the training institution and the appropriate professional body.

(d) *Length of Professional Training:*

This professional training should last for at least *two full years* and from the outset should be both practical and theoretical. It is desirable that theoretical training should predominate in the first year backed however by diversified practical experience (in schools, clinics, etc.). The second year should lay greater stress upon practical training, particularly upon work in a psychological service under the supervision of an experienced educational psychologist.

(e) *Content and Method of Professional Training:*

It is inappropriate here to enter into details of training. The committee however suggests that this should be balanced between courses covering systematic theory, practical work, and continuous periods of supervised practice. The educational psychologist should come to understand the structure of groups as well as the psychology of individuals. He should be fully trained in child development, the psychology of subject matter, in observational techniques, in tests and measurements, in experimental and research design, and in remedial methods of all kinds, so that he may give educational guidance, conduct psychological examinations, undertake remedial work and co-operate in or carry out research.

PROFESSIONAL RESPONSIBILITY

In few countries as yet have educational psychologists a legally protected professional status other than that conferred upon them by their teaching function. In many however the specialization has been administratively recognized and a de facto status acquired. This committee urges on the attention of responsible bodies (notably Ministries of Education) the need for establishing jointly with the profession, a professional code and an adequate register of those competent to practise. As an interim measure, pending legal sanction, a council of the profession itself should invite the participation of the teaching profession, the educational administration and possibly of allied professions working in closely related fields, in the setting up and control of training standards and the granting of professional recognition to newly trained psychologists.

One of the more important items in any professional code will be that related to professional discretion and confidence. The psychologist by the very nature of his function receives confidential information from parents, teachers and children. He will also through his professional investigation discover facts concerning individuals, their personality, background, capacities and the like which, while necessary to the formation of an adequate opinion, should not in their crude form be divulged to those not competent to interpret them. Thus only such information as is in the best interests of the child, should be passed on to colleagues in other professions, and this information should be transmitted in a form which is intelligible to them. Detailed case material, the results of psychological tests and the like should not be generally divulged. Only in this way can the psychologist observe a professional code of ethics and justify the confidence reposed in him by all concerned. Where the psychologist is acting primarily as consultant to the teacher he is naturally under a special obligation to inform his colleague of all that is directly relevant to the teacher's task and responsibility vis à vis the child, without of course abandoning his duty to observe the confidence reposed in him by the parents or by the child.

SUMMARY AND CONCLUSIONS

The main preoccupation of the educational psychologist is with the child; and the main object of a school psychological service is to aid the school in ensuring the fullest possible development of each child's personality in consonance with the needs of his society. It is a shortsighted policy to confine a psychological service, deliberately or by shortage of staff, finance or promises, solely to the task of detecting and treating maladjusted or failing children. Active prevention of educational, social or emotional disturbance and constructive amelioration of the school and home environment of children are less costly in the long run (socially and financially) than the treatment of cases which have been allowed to develop to the point where something drastic must be done. Thus though remedial work of all kinds is an essential part of a comprehensive psychological service for schools, the primary aim should be constructive and preventive mental hygiene.

The committee wishes to underline that, to bring about the most favourable educational climate, the methods and curricula of schools must be adapted to the rhythms of child growth and to individual differences. The whole class and school atmosphere moreover must deeply satisfy the child's need for human contacts. The individualization of method and still more the change from an impersonal or repressive discipline to a freer, more natural atmosphere in the classroom may well raise difficulties for the teacher or provoke temporary problems in the children themselves which are not easy for teachers to handle. Through continuing research, through bringing psychological knowledge to bear on the initial and further training of teachers, and through collaboration with teachers over particular cases, the educational psychologist can contribute fundamentally to the solution of these problems, and bring about that improvement in education which is the best means of preventing maladjustments.

Many problems of development originate in the child's out-of-school life. Hence a psychological service must concern itself directly with the families and with the total environment of children, aiding generally in parent education and, where necessary, attempting to modify the attitudes of parents to children whose difficulties are rooted in mishandling at home. This latter task is particularly important where some remedial action is undertaken with an individual problem child who may for example be sent to a special class or for a period placed in a special school. Any remedial or therapeutic measure of this kind risks failure if it is applied to the child only and no attempt made to change causal factors in the environment.

The continuing and objective study of all children, carried out by teachers themselves helped by the psychologist, is the basis of sound educational guidance. Where this exists, problem cases are detected early and more intensive studies of maladjusted, failing or handicapped children fall into their rightful place against a background of normality. It is perhaps unnecessary to state that such studies, whether the cumulative records of the teacher or the more intensive and deep study of the psychologist, should not aim at a kind of catalogue of personality traits or at attaching diagnostic labels. The full examinations carried out by the psychologist aim to evaluate and understand, not merely the results of tests of various kinds, but data derived from an investigation of all aspects of the child's life, his social relationships in the family, school and out-of-school environments, his intellectual and emotional reactions, his state of physical health and development. Such a dynamic study involves the whole personality and training of the psychologist and is not a matter for those who have acquired a little knowledge of mental tests. The blind application of tests by those untrained in their use and the conception current in some quarters that the work of a psychologist should be confined to psychometrics cannot be too strongly deprecated. It is for this reason that the committee insists upon a broad and thorough training for the psychologist, a full freedom of professional action and the necessary protection of the conditions of confidence and responsibility.

The psychologist however cannot function alone; nor can a psychological service confine itself to an advisory rôle for the teachers of children of school age. This implies that many other types of work and service are needed which should be functionally integrated with the constructive and preventive work carried out in the schools. Services such as remedial education, some forms of special educational provision, schools for the maladjusted, child guidance centres for treatment of problem cases and the like should form a part of the psychological service; with others, for example services of social welfare and school medical services, the psychologist should act as liaison. Similarly since the aim of a psychological service for children is to be comprehensive and to ensure what assistance is necessary from the pre-school period to the time when the adolescent is fully integrated into adult life, no pains should be spared to ensure close co-operation between all those services which are in contact with the family and with the work environment. The current fragmentation of administrative and financial responsibility which leads to overlapping on the one hand and to gaps on the other, should be resolutely overcome in the best interests of all children.

The basis of constructive work for the all-round development of children is multi-disciplined; that is to suggest in practice the team of specialists each with a distinctive contribution to make. Such teams will be differently constituted to meet different needs and will vary in the kind of service—advisory, diagnostic or remedial—they are called upon to provide. Their effectiveness, for whatever purpose and however constituted, depends upon inter-professional co-operation in the real sense, and this can be achieved only if each member respects the insight and knowledge of the others and if there is a common understanding of professional responsibility. It is for this reason that the committee recommends that all workers concerned with the mental, emotional and social wellbeing of children should in their training be given some acquaintance with specialities other than their own; and that as much as possible of the training of those who make up child guidance and similar teams should be conjoint.

BIBLIOGRAPHY

I, PSYCHOLOGICAL SERVICES

ALEXANDER, W. P., *The Child Guidance Service in Principle and in Fact*. Sheffield, Education Committee, 1943.

BLACKER, C. P., *Neurosis and the Mental Health Services*. Oxford. Oxford University Press, 1946.

BOESCH, E., *L'organisation d'un service de psychologie scolaire*. St-Gall, Tschudy, 1946.

Bruxelles, *Du Service social scolaire. Projet De Coster–Weber*. Impr. G.I.C., Bruxelles, 1948.

BUCK, J. & ANSELME, FR., *Centres d'orientation scolaire et professionnelle de la jeunesse*. Malonne, Nouvelle Revue Pédagogique, 1951.

DE COSTER, S., *Le développement du Service Social Scolaire*. Bruxelles, Le Service Social, 1952.

DERIVIERE, R., "Un Centre psycho-médico-social de l'enseignement moyen." *Revue Belge de Psychologie et de Pédagogie*, Cahier XII, Bruxelles, 1951.

ERICKSON, C. E. & SMITH, G. E., *Organisation and Administration of Guidance Services*. New York and London, McGraw-Hill Book Company, 1947.

JADOULLE, A., *Le laboratoire pédagogique au travail*. Paris, Centres d'Entraînement aux Méthodes d'Education active, Les Editions du Scarabée, 1951.

LAFON, R., *Psycho-pédagogie médico-sociale*. Paris, Presses Universitaires de France, 1950.

LAUBE, FR., *Wesen und Aufgaben der Erziehungsberatung*. Solothurn, St. Antoniusverlag, 1953.

Liste des organismes de dépistage et de rééducation de mineurs inadaptés. Paris, Union nationale des Associations régionales, 1954.

OSTERRIETH, P., *Le centre médico-psychologique pour enfants et adolescents*. Bruxelles, Revue du centre neuro-psychiatrique, 1947.

SCHONELL, F. J. & WALL, W. D., "The Remedial Education Centre", *Educational Review*, Vol. II, no. I, 1949.

WALL, W. D., "Psychological Services for Children in Europe", *Yearbook of Education*, London, Evans Bros., 1955.

WITMER, H. L., *Psychiatric Clinics for Children*. Oxford, Oxford University Press, 1940.

ZAZZO, R., GRATIOT–ALPHANDERY, H., "La psychologie scolaire". *Enfance*, Vol. 5, no. 5, Nov.–Dec. 1952.

II. PSYCHOLOGISTS

CLARK, K., "The APA Study of Psychologists" *Amer. Psychology*, 1954, 9, 3, Mar, 117–120.

CUTTS, N. E., (Ed.) *School Psychologists at Mid-Century*. Washington, 1955.

DANIEL, R. S., LOUTTIT, C. M., *Professional Problems in Psychology*. New-York Prentice-Hall, 1953.

KELLY, *Training in Clinical Psychology*. New-York Prentice-Hall, 1950.

KENNEDY, A., DAVIDSON, M., KEIR, G., McCALLUM, C. M., MOODY, R. L., BANKS, C., BURT, C., "Symposium on Psychologists and Psychiatrists in the Child Guidance Service", *British Journal Psychology*, Vol. XXI, XXII, XXXIII, 1951–1953.

Les psychologues scolaires. Paris, Unesco; Geneva, Bureau International d'Education, Publication no. 104, 1948.

School Psychologists. Paris, Unesco; Geneva, International Bureau of Education, Publication no. 105, 1948.

III. EDUCATIONAL GUIDANCE

ALDERBLUM, E., "Beginning School-Guidance early". *Mental Hygiene*, U.S.A., Vol. 34, no. 4, Oct. 1950.

BERTIER, G., *L'orientation professionnelle de la jeunesse bourgeoise*. Paris, Téqui, 1940.

CASSIDY, R. & KOZMAN, H. CL., Foreword by MEAD, M., *Counseling Girls in a Changing Society*, New York & London, McGraw-Hill Book Co., 1947.

CLEUGH, M. F., *Psychology in the Service of the School*. London, Methuen, 1951.

ERICKSON, C. E. & SMITH, G. E., *Organization and Administration of Guidance Services*. New York & London, McGraw-Hill Book Co., 1947.

GAL, R., *L'orientation scolaire*. Paris, Presses Universitaires de France, 1946.

HAMLEY et al., *The Educational Guidance of the School Child*. London, Evans Bros., 1937.

LITTLE, W. & CHAPMAN, A. L., *Developmental Guidance in Secondary School*. New York, Toronto & London, McGraw-Hill Book Co., 1953.

STRANG, R., *Educational Guidance: Its Principles and Pratice*. New York, McMillan, 1948.

UNIVERSITA CATTOLICA DEL S. CUORE, *Contributi del Laboratorio di psicologia*. Serie undecima. GASTLIGLIONI, G., *Saggio di analisi delle attiduni e tendenze di scolari mediante reattivi ai fini dell'orientamento professionale*. Milano, "Vita e Pensiero", 1943-XXI.

WITMER, M. & PROFFITT, M., *Guidance Bibliography*. Washington, U.S. Department of the Interior, Office of Education, Bulletin 1937, no. 37.

WRENN, C. G. & DUGAN, W. E., *Guidance Procedures in High School; Some Recommended Procedures Based upon a Survey of Present Practices in Minnesota*. University of Minnesota. College of Education. Modern school practices series no. I. Minneapolis, U. of Minnesota P., 1950.

IV. SCHOOL RECORDS CARD

FLEMING, C. M., *Cumulative Records: Notes on their Content and Uses*. London, University of London Press, 1945.

GLASSEY, W., *The Educational Development of Children; the Teacher's Guide to the Keeping of School Records*. London, 1950.

KIENZLE, R., *Schülerbeobachtung and Schülerbeurteilung*. Esslingen/a/N., Schneider, 1949.

LANG, L., *Neue Wege zur Schülerkenntnis*. Wien, Oesterreichischer Bundesverlag für Unterricht, Wissenschaft und Kunst, 1950.

V. VOCATIONAL GUIDANCE

BUREAU INTERNATIONAL DU TRAVAIL, *L'orientation professionnelle*. Geneva, Bureau international du Travail, 1947.

DIVISIONE STATISTICA E LAVORO DELLA CITA DI TORINO, *Atti del I⁰ congresso nazionale di orientamento professionale*. Torino 11-14 sept. 1948, Tipografia Gattiglia, 1949.

EDWARDS, R., *Vocational and Occupational Guidance*. Cambridge, Heffer, 1940.

"Die Eignungsuntersuchung im Dienste der Berufswahl". Zürich, Sonderdruck aus der Zeitschrift, *Berufsberatung und Berufsbildung*, 1947, Nr. 1/2.

Une expérience d'orientation. Ministère Education Nationale, France, 1954.

FITCH, J., *Vocational Guidance in Action*. New York, Columbia University Press; London, Oxford University Press, 1935.

GEMELLI, A., *L'orientamento professionale dei giovani nelle scuole*. Milano, "Vita e Pensiero", 1947.

HUNT, E. P. & SMITH, P., *Scientific Vocational Guidance and its value to the choice of employment work of a Local Education Authority*. Birmingham, City of Birmingham Education Committee, Nov. 1944.

INTERNATIONAL LABOUR OFFICE, *Vocational Guidance*. Geneva, International Labour Office, 1947.

KELLER, F. J. & VITELES, M. S., *Vocational Guidance throughout the World*. London, Jonathan Cape, 1937.

MCQUEEN, H. C. & others., *The Background of Guidance*. Wellington, New Zealand Council for Educational Research, 1941.

MACRAE, A., *The Case for Vocational Guidance*. Pitman, London, 1934.

MALLART, J., *La orientación profesional y la escuela*. Publicado en la Revista Española de Pedagogía (tomo II, num. 5) del Instituto San José de Calasanz. Madrid, 1944.

MEILI, R., *Psychologie de l'orientation professionnelle*. Geneva, Editions du Mont-Blanc, 1948.

MIRA Y LOPEZ, E., *Manual de orientación profesional*. Buenos-Aires, Kapelusz, 1947.

THE NATIONAL ADVISORY COUNCIL FOR JUVENILE EMPLOYMENT, *England and Wales, and Scotland. Joint Report on the Organisation and Development of the Vocational Guidance Service in Great Britain*, 1934. H.M. Stationery Office, London.

L'orientation professionnelle. Numéro spécial de "Educateurs", juillet-août 1947. Service central de Recherche et d'Action pour l'Enfance; 31 rue de Fleurus, Paris.

ROYAUME DE BELGIQUE. MINISTERE DE L'INSTRUCTION PUBLIQUE, *Service de l'orientation professionnelle. Informations*. Bruxelles, Ministère de l'Instruction publique, 1949.

LIST OF MEMBERS
EXPERT STUDY GROUP ON PSYCHOLOGICAL
SERVICES FOR SCHOOLS

Unesco Institute for Education,
Hamburg, 5–10 April, 1954

THE UNITED NATIONS TECHNICAL ASSISTANCE ADMIN-ISTRATION, EUROPEAN OFFICE

Miss G. MEYERAND, Fulbright Professor of Social Work, Pierce College, Elleniko (Greece)	UNITED STATES
Miss D. RÖNNQVIST, School Social Worker, Stockholm	SWEDEN

UNESCO

Dr. E. BOESCH, Professor of Psychology, Unversity of Sarrebrück (Rapporteur)	SAAR
Miss M. B. DAVIDSON, Secretary of the Committee of Professional Psychologists, British Psychological Society	UNITED KINGDOM
Dr. F. HOTYAT, Director of the Centre de Travaux of the Institut Supérieur de Pédagogie du Hainaut, Morlanwelz (Rapporteur)	BELGIUM
M. R. ZAZZO, Director of the Laboratoire de Psycho-biologie de l'Enfant, Paris	FRANCE

WORLD HEALTH ORGANIZATION, EUROPEAN OFFICE

Dr. H. M. COHEN, School Medical Officer, City of Birmingham	UNITED KINGDOM
Dr. W. DEUCHLER, School Medical Officer, Zurich	SWITZERLAND

WORLD FEDERATION FOR MENTAL HEALTH

The Lady NORMAN, Vice-President, World Federation for Mental Health (Chairman)	UNITED KINGDOM

UNESCO INSTITUTE FOR EDUCATION

Dr. MÄRTA BJÖRSJÖ, Royal Board of Education, Stockholm	SWEDEN

Dr. C. Bondy, Professor of Psychology and Social Pedagogics, University of Hamburg (Vice-Chairman)　GERMANY

M. R. Gal, Conseiller technique pédagogique du Ministère de l'Education nationale, Chargé du Service de la recherche pédagogique, Paris　FRANCE

Dr. G. Geissler, Professor of Education and Director of the Educational Institute, University of Hamburg　GERMANY

Dr. M. Keilhacker, Professor of Psychology and Education ,University of Munich　GERMANY

† Dr. O. Kroh, Professor of Education and Psychology, Free University of Berlin　GERMANY

Dr. H. Möhring, Head, Department of Social and Remedial Education, Educational Institute, University of Hamburg　GERMANY

Dr. H. Schulte, Professor of Psychiatry, Bremen　GERMANY

Dr. M. Simmen, School Psychological Service, Lucerne　SWITZERLAND

M. G. Sinoir, Psychologue attaché à la Direction de l'Education Surveillée au Ministère de la Justice, Paris　FRANCE

SECRETARIAT

Miss U. M. Gallusser, Department of Education, Unesco, Paris

Mr. C. R. E. Gillett, Deputy Director, Unesco Institute for Education, Hamburg

Professor W. Merck, Director, Unesco Institute for Education, Hamburg

Dr. W. D. Wall, Department of Education, Unesco, Paris

† Deceased, 11 September, 1955

PUBLICATIONS IN THIS SERIES

This booklet is No. 3 of the *Unesco Institute for Education Publications*; it is also one of a series of publications concerning **education and the mental health of children,** which includes studies published either by UNESCO itself or by certain non-governmental organisations in collaboration with UNESCO.

A. UNESCO INSTITUTE FOR EDUCATION PUBLICATIONS

No. 1   *Adult Education towards Social and Political Responsibility.* Ed. Frank W. Jessup—Hamburg, 1953. 144 pp. $ 0.75; DM 2.50; ffrs. 100; 3/6 (English and French)

No. 2   *Kleinkinderziehung in Familie und Kindergarten.* Ed. Agnes Niegl —Hamburg, 1954. 180 pp. $ 1.00; DM 3.00; ffrs. 300; 5/- (German only).

B. EDUCATION AND MENTAL HEALTH OF CHILDREN SERIES

Already published:

Mental Hygiene in the Nursery School — Paris, Unesco, 1955. 35 pp. 1/-; ffrs. 50; $ 0.20; (English and French)

Training of Teachers. Conference of Internationally-Minded Schools, Mr. Frank Button (Secretary), 5, Warwick Road, Reading, Berks, England, 1955. 50 pp. approx. (English and French).

Education and Mental Health, by W. D. Wall, Paris, Unesco, 1955. 347 pp. ffrs. 650; 13/6; $ 2.50 paper; 17/6; $ 3.00; ffrs 850 cloth bound. (English and French).

La Pédagogie du Calcul. Ecole Normale supérieure de Saint-Cloud (Seine & Oise), France, 1955, 50 pp. approx. (French only).

The Police and the Mental Health of Children, International Federation of Senior Police Officers, 11 rue des Saussaies, Paris, 8ème, 54 pp. 2/-; ffrs 100; $ 0.35 post free (English and French).

Periods of Tension in the Primary School. National Association for Mental Health, 29 Queen Anne Street, London W.C.1. 1955 (English and French). 38 pp. 3/-; ffrs 150; $ 0.55.